DEADLY DIMITAR

CHRIS DAVIES

DEADLY
DIMITAR

THE BIOGRAPHY OF SUPERSTRIKER
DIMITAR BERBATOV

JOHN BLAKE

Published by John Blake Publishing Ltd,
3 Bramber Court, 2 Bramber Road,
London W14 9PB, England

www.johnblakepublishing.co.uk

First published in hardback in 2009

ISBN: 978-1-84454-569-8

British Library Cataloguing-in-Publication Data:

A catalogue record for this book is available from the British Library.

Design by www.envydesign.co.uk

Printed in the UK by CPI William Clowes Beccles NR34 7TL

1 3 5 7 9 10 8 6 4 2

Papers used by John Blake Publishing are natural,
recyclable products made from wood grown in sustainable forests.
The manufacturing processes conform to the environmental
regulations of the country of origin.

Every attempt has been made to contact the relevant copyright-holders,
but some were unobtainable. We would be grateful if the appropriate
people could contact us.

Photos © Getty Images, Cleva Media and PA Photos

CONTENTS

CHAPTER 1

RED DEVIL WITH AN ANGEL'S FACE

'I find myself sitting at home sometimes, thinking – Hey, I am at Manchester United! I am the happiest guy. It is a wonderful thing.'
DIMITAR BERBATOV

O ver the past century the eastern-bloc has developed a reputation as a breeding ground for some of the most technically gifted footballers the world has ever seen. Names such as Puskas, Blokhin, Yashin, Lato, Hagi, Stoichkov and Shevchenko are synonymous with eastern European football and they are among the greatest players to have ever emerged from the region. And, at the speed with which Manchester United forward Dimitar Berbatov is progressing in his career, it surely won't be too long before the talented Bulgarian, already a hero in his homeland, is mentioned in the same breath as such illustrious company.

During his time in England, he has been unjustly accused by the ever-critical English media of being lethargic, lazy and lackadaisical. Indeed, when he signed for Tottenham Hotspur in the summer of 2006, his former manager at Bayer Leverkusen, Klaus Toppmoller seemed to endorse that view. They are accusations that Berbatov knows to be unfounded: 'I may not run non-stop, because there is no need to chase unreachable balls.' It is difficult to argue with his view given the amount of goals he has scored and match-winning performances he has supplied during his first two-and-a-half seasons in England with both Spurs and Manchester United. Initially, he took time, as most foreign imports do, to adapt to his new surroundings and teammates. But after finding his feet, he went on to forge a lethal partnership, one of the best in the Premiership with fellow striker Robbie Keane, netting 23 goals in all competitions in his first season in North London. Not bad for a new arrival given the difference in pace and style between the German and English leagues.

In one season, his exciting style of play, an array of wonder goals and his love of playing beautiful football endeared him to the appreciative Spurs faithful. You see, Spurs fans love nothing more than exciting football played by exciting players. And after witnessing an array of his sultry skills they were left in no doubt that manager, Martin Jol, had unearthed a diamond in the mould of Hoddle, Gascoigne, Ginola et al. He was the new darling of the fans; their new idol; their saviour. 'The devil with the face of an angel' as he was nicknamed in Germany because his innocent appearance was offset by a deadly ability to score goals, was the latest in a long line of players at Spurs who really could play the 'beautiful game' the way it was meant to be played.

Unsurprisingly, after settling in to the English way of

life and the trials and tribulations of the Premiership with aplomb, Berbatov found himself the subject of intense transfer speculation at the end of his first season at White Hart Lane. The summer of 2007 and the subsequent mid-season transfer window in January 2008 saw the broadsheet newspapers as guilty of tipping the speculation to fever pitch as their red-top peers. Teams of the stature and financial muscle of Manchester United and Chelsea were continually linked to possible multi-million pound bids to take the gifted eastern-European forward away from north London, while headline after headline reported that the Bulgarian wanted to move on to bigger and better things.

Despite the never-ending media frenzy surrounding his future, Berbatov remained silent on the issue until the speculation rose to a level he felt warranted a response. Feeling the need to quash the rumours and the concerns of the supporters who were loathe to see him swap the famous white shirt of their team for the blue of their west London compatriots or the red of their northern rivals, as former Spur Michael Carrick had done in the summer of 2006, Berbatov revealed his thoughts.

In early January 2008, he attempted to reassure the fans that his heart was still in north London when he told the Bulgarian television station *Nova TV*: 'There are too many speculations around my name, but most of them are foolish. It's absurd and I'm tired of seeing my name in the newspapers. I want to live in peace. It is getting too much. I am a Tottenham player and I'm trying to give my best, so I can help my team. I'm happy when we play well and I'm miserable when we lose our games. I'm happy at the moment. You can win titles and medals with every team and I can win with Tottenham too.'

When the interview filtered through to the English media it was music to the ears of the Lilywhites' faithful, who after Martin Jol's controversial departure in October 2007, were looking to his replacement, Juande Ramos, to steady the ship and deliver the trophies they craved. Having their star striker on board and happy to remain a Spur would surely only improve their chances of landing such silverware.

Unlike a number of his peers, the six-foot-two striker is not your archetypal footballer on or indeed off the pitch. Despite his celebrity status and large pay packet, he doesn't strive to make the headlines in the tabloids. Headlines about this very private footballer are confined to the back pages rather than the front covers and gossip pages. And despite arriving in England with a reputation for enjoying the finer side of life and trips to local nightclubs during his time in Germany, Berbatov prefers instead to shun the media spotlight and keep his private life to himself.

Ulrich Dost, Leverkusen's press officer admitted that Berbatov was often reluctant to speak to the media about life outside football during his time in Germany, preferring instead to avoid interviews in general wherever possible: 'He didn't like giving interviews. You virtually had to force him to do it. And when he did, he only talked about football. He never discussed his private life.'

In an interview with *The Times* in June 2007, Berbatov's mother Margarita, who is the head of nursing at Blagoevgrad city hospital, revealed a private and compassionate side of Berbatov that is rarely seen. During his first season at Spurs, he sported an armband in the white, green and red colours of his national flag with the slogan 'You are not alone' emblazoned on it, to show his support for five Bulgarian nurses sentenced to death in Libya for allegations of spreading the HIV virus. His mother, who is spearheading the campaign for the release of the five captives, who strongly oppose the accusations, said: 'I had no idea Mitko [Dimitar's nickname] was going to join the campaign. It was his idea, but he has always supported my work. I was watching him play for Spurs one weekend and there was the armband. It made me so proud. It was natural for Mitko to wear the band. He is a very compassionate man and football is not the only thing in his life. Whenever he is here, he comes with me to the orphanage I support and brings them gifts. Now the children all have shoes because of him. They love him.'

Berbatov had arrived in England as Tottenham's new £10.9 million star signing from Bayer Leverkusen after five-and-a-half seasons in the Rhineland region of western Germany. During his time at the Bay Arena – Leverkusen's stadium – he had assumed the role of the darling of the Leverkusen fans after finishing as the club's top goal scorer in his last three seasons with them. His signing for Spurs also coincided with his appointment as Bulgaria's UNICEF goodwill ambassador for disabled children. Speaking at the subsequent press conference, Bulgarian news agency www.novinite.com quoted Berbatov as saying: 'I am proud to be a part of that organisation. I would like to use my popularity and to lobby for the rights of these children and to seek reforms that would ease their life. My dreams have already become reality, now I want to help these children start dreaming.'

He continued by voicing his determination to do all in his power to help disabled children integrate into Bulgarian society and into a normal life in his home country: 'I would like to say that I am glad and above all proud to be now part of the family of this organisation, which takes care of what is most important in our world – the children. Kids would always be the future of this country and the world. That is why as a goodwill ambassador I will be helping with anything I can. I would be lobbying for the observance of disabled children's rights, who are quite high in number in Bulgaria. We don't see them in the streets, in the sports and playgrounds at school. I hope to be able to help the children of Bulgaria and especially disabled children not to feel in danger or threatened of being mocked but to know they are part of us all in Bulgaria.'

On the international front Berbatov is a legend within his own country. He has scored a remarkable 41 goals in just 67 internationals in the green and white kit of Bulgaria since making his debut for the national team in a friendly against Chile in 1999. That is more than the legendary Hristo Stoichkov and second only in the top goal-scorer standings to former national team star and manager Hristo Bonev, who tucked away 47 goals in 96 appearances. With a ratio of more than a goal every other game it is surely only a matter of time before he overtakes Bonev's long-standing record. Berbatov was also awarded the ultimate honour of the national team captaincy by the then coach, Stoichkov in March 2007, who said: 'Berbatov has proved his excellent quality of a team leader. He makes goals and helps the whole squad as well.'

However, Bulgaria's captain has only had the honour of representing his country at one international tournament since he made his debut in 1999, when in 2004 Bulgaria disappointingly lost all three games at the European Championships in Portugal. It is an unwelcome statistic that Berbatov will be hoping to rectify as he leads his countrymen into the qualifying matches for the 2010 World Cup to be held in South Africa. But, if Berbatov is to represent his country in the world's greatest showpiece event, he will need to help his colleagues past the challenge of a tough group consisting of Italy, Republic of Ireland, Cyprus, Georgia and Montenegro. After drawing each of their opening three matches in the qualifying stages thus far, the prolific forward will need the help of his less talented teammates if he is to fulfil perhaps his last opportunity to play in a World Cup.

After a stunning first season with Spurs, Berbatov entered into his second season with questions being asked about his ability to repeat his debut season form for the club and help them progress into a Champions League qualifying position, after two fifth place finishes in succession. Following a less than auspicious start to the new season, both from a personal point of view and for the team in general, Berbatov helped inspire Spurs and their new Spanish manager Juande Ramos to win the final of the Carling Cup at the New Wembley, beating North London rivals Arsenal en route in the semi-finals before defeating Chelsea courtesy of a penalty from Berbatov and a winning goal from Jonathan Woodgate. Having witnessed his contribution to ending the club's nine-year wait for a trophy, Tottenham's fans hoped he would maintain his stance about believing he could win things at the Lane.

Unfortunately for them though, after completing his second season at Spurs with a total of 23 goals in all competitions for the second season running, Berbatov's head was ultimately turned by the admiring glances coming his way from Manchester United's Sir Alex Ferguson. The opportunity to move to one of the world's biggest clubs; to play at United's self-acclaimed *Theatre of Dreams*; to regularly challenge for the biggest prizes in football year in year out and to follow in the footsteps of some of the game's biggest stars such as Charlton, Best, Giggs and Cantona would be a tough one for anyone to turn down. And despite Tottenham's best efforts to persuade their talismanic star to commit his future to the club, United's mammoth offer of £30.75 million on transfer deadline day in September 2008 for a player whose heart was clearly no longer white, saw Berbatov depart White Hart Lane for the Red Devils in search of more silverware and ultimately the one thing Spurs could not offer him, Champions League football.

CHAPTER 2

IN THE BEGINNING...

'Some are born great, some achieve greatness, and some have greatness thrust upon them.'
WILLIAM SHAKESPEARE, *TWELFTH NIGHT*

Every once in a while, every country, from the largest to the smallest, the richest to the poorest, and in every corner of the globe, produces a sportsman or woman of unique skill and talent. Some 28 years ago in the small south-west town of Blagoevgrad – known previously as Gorna Dzhumaya until 1950 and situated within the province of Pirin – one such footballer – Dimitar Ivanov Berbatov – was born into communist Bulgaria.

Born on 30 January 1981, Berbatov shares his birthday with the lanky Portsmouth and England international striker and fellow former Spur, Peter Crouch. He came from a sporting background, with his mother, Margarita, a former handball player, and his father Ivan, a former footballer with hometown club Pirin Blagoevgrad and CSKA Sofia. Life in Bulgaria during the communist regime wasn't easy for anybody. In an insightful interview with the *Sunday Mirror* in September 2007, Berbatov junior revealed the difficulties of his childhood life due to a lack of money in the country, but also in contrast, the affinity he felt of being part of a close family:

'There was no money in my country. It was a time of great depression. But it was the same for everyone. We had nothing to spend on food, let alone something we liked. Even if we wanted bread we had to wait in line for seven or eight hours. We would have to get in line at six in the morning, and if you lost your place in the line you had to go to the back. But we knew no different – there was nothing to compare it with. When you are growing up you don't realise there is another life somewhere else.

'Six of us lived in a one-bedroom flat. I lived with my parents, grandparents and brother, and I would sleep on the sofa. But strangely, I miss it in some ways. I had my friends and the conditions unite and strengthen you. My whole personality has been shaped by my upbringing.

'Am I bitter? No. Hardship builds your character – I don't look back on it with anger. But I know what a crisis is. I know what it's like to make sacrifices. I appreciate life and I never take anything for granted. I could never look back and say I was an unhappy boy. I wasn't.'

As a schoolboy, Berbatov – better known as 'Mitko' to his family and friends – acquired a passion for art, and in particular drawing, which he has retained to the current day. Nevertheless, despite his love of sketching, it was in the world of sport that the young Dimitar excelled, rather than in the classroom. An enthusiastic and talented athlete, his favoured disciplines included the long jump and running, but any passion he may have had for athletics paled into insignificance when it came to playing football. The first ball he ever received was a basketball, yet all he wanted to do was kick the ball with his feet like Bulgarian football legend Hristo Stoichkov, rather than bounce it and throw it through a basketball hoop like American basketball legend Michael Jordan.

Henceforth, having displayed a talent for the game, he was, at the age of just 10-years-old, admitted into the Blagoevgrad Academy of football – a well-renowned school of football for young hopefuls in the province of Pirin. His dream of becoming a professional footballer had begun. It was now down to him, with the guidance of the Academy's coaches and his father, to progress and improve if he wanted to take his chance and make his dream a reality. As a child, having shown an aptitude for goalscoring, Berbatov's father, Ivan, taught his son the basics of forward play that he admits have stayed with him to the current day. In an interview with *The Times* in May 2007, Berbatov revealed how his father had been a big influence on the way he plays the game today, and how he still regularly talks to him about his performances and ways in which he can improve his game:

'We discuss how not to make the same mistakes. For example, when I miss, don't control the ball, shoot or pass. I listen to him. I try to do the best not to disappoint him. If I can make my parents proud, I am a successful man. He tells me good things, too. When I was younger, sometimes I thought, "Why is he talking like that?" But as time went by I started to realise he was right. When he wanted to be critical, he did not say, "You stupid this or that". He encouraged me to try to do this next time.'

During Berbatov's early teenage years, Bulgarian football experienced its golden period; a period it had never before and has never since come close to eclipsing. The national team – inspired by players of the stature and calibre of superstar striker Hristo Stoichkov, who plied his trade in the Spanish league with Catalan giants Barcelona, and midfielders Krassimir Balakov and Yordan Lechkov – shocked the world of football by reaching the semi-final stage of the 1994 World Cup in the United States. The tournament had begun awfully for the team, as the *Super Eagles* from Nigeria – who were making their tournament debut – dismantled them 4-0 in their opening match.

The team bounced back with a stylish 4-0 drubbing of Greece, before defeating one of the perennial pre-tournament favourites, Argentina 2-0 – minus Diego Maradona, who had been banned following his country's previous game after failing a random drug test – to rubber-stamp qualification for the knock out stages of the tournament. A 1-1 draw after extra time with Mexico in the second round meant the game would be decided by penalties. Bulgaria kept their nerve to win through 2-0 and set up a fascinating, yet daunting first ever quarter-final with World Cup veterans Germany.

Despite the Germans' tag as overwhelming favourites to win the game and progress to the semi-finals, goals from the inspirational Stoichkov and the now famous bald head of Lechkov, won the game for Bulgaria – one of the biggest shocks still in World Cup history. The team lost narrowly in the semi-final to an Italian team carried by Roberto Baggio, and then again in the third/fourth play-off against Sweden. But despite the defeats, they had made the rest of the world sit up and take notice of Bulgarian football. Prior to that World Cup the nation had never before won a match in the finals.

The unexpected success of the 'golden generation', as they became known, served as an inspiration to the country's young footballers, Berbatov included, as he revealed to *The Observer* in 2007: 'We will never forget it because that was the time that made our generation believe we could do something in football – maybe do the same as them.'

However, while growing up, rather than idolising one of Bulgaria's top players of the time such as Stoichkov or Balakov, Berbatov admits to having revered two strikers from outside his country. 'When I was young I really liked Marco van Basten and Alan Shearer and when we were playing and I got the ball I would say those names. When you grow up you think you were a bit silly, but when you look back at those times they were very special,' he told a Tottenham Hotspur match day programme in May 2007.

As a teenager, Berbatov had received a Newcastle United shirt for his birthday one year from his doting parents, adorned with Shearer's famous number nine on the back and his own surname above it. The shirt became his prized possession and his mother Margarita revealed in *The Sun* how it strengthened his adulation for Shearer and Newcastle: 'Dimitar wore this shirt all the time. He even used to sleep in his Newcastle shirt! It's that special to him. Dimitar told me it was his dream to play for Newcastle United one day and wear the same shirt as

Alan Shearer, who is my son's hero. Shearer was a major inspiration for him to work hard for himself and the team. He liked the fact that Alan Shearer scored goals but was not a selfish player. Dimitar thinks this shirt may even have been a sign he was meant to play in England.'

And at the age of just 17 years old, he made the first tentative steps of his fledgling career and towards his dream of an eventual move to England. Following in his father's footsteps, he turned out for his hometown club, Pirin Blagoevgrad. Yet, within a season, his progress and obvious talent had been noticed by one of Bulgaria's biggest and most famous clubs, CSKA Sofia, and their legendary coach, Dimitar Penev, who had managed Bulgaria to their fourth place finish in the 1994 World Cup. Penev spotted him playing in the colours of Pirin and offered him the opportunity of a trial with the famous old army club from the country's capital city.

CSKA and Penev had identified Berbatov as one of a number of talented teenagers that they wanted to spearhead their assault on the league championship after losing the title they had won in 1997 to the newly promoted team, Litex Lovech. And, after impressing CSKA's management team during his trial period, he was offered the chance to sign professionally for the club. Once again, Berbatov junior was following the path that his father had taken during his own career as a forward-cum-defender. He left his family and friends to begin his adventure in the famous red kit of CSKA, some 100 kilometres north of his home in Blagoevgrad.

Amusingly, the cost of his transfer to CSKA totalled a lowly £3,000 and 20 pairs of football boots. In an interview with the *Sunday Mirror* in September 2007, Berbatov revealed his amusement at the size of his transfer from Pirin: 'I didn't find out about it until later on. But I think it's important to be able to laugh at yourself and not take life so seriously. So they paid 20 pairs of boots for me. It's funny, isn't it?'

Later in his career, he praised Penev – who had also discovered Stoichkov as a youngster – in *The Times*, for giving him his shot at the big time: 'I will forever be thankful to Dimitar Penev. When he first phoned me and said he was interested in me, I did not hesitate. It was Dimitar Penev! The very next day, I had a trial at CSKA.'

Although he had joined the biggest club in the country, a club which had won a record 28 championships at the time, Berbatov's time at CSKA was far from luxurious, a million miles away from the situation he finds himself in today at Manchester United as one of the Premier League's top players and high earners. Speaking to the *Daily Telegraph* in November 2006, he explained the situation that he and other fellow young team-mates who had been bought in from other regions of the country had found themselves in at their new club. Living in dormitories and given little money to spend, he explained how that helped them forge closer relationships with one another:

'We had a very hard time. It was difficult, not just for me but for all my team-mates. In the national team now, there are six or seven players who were all together in the under-21s and before that at CSKA. We know how we got where we are and we will never forget that. Sometimes we talk about how it was and how it is now.

That makes us very close. First we are friends and then team-mates after.'

He made his debut for the first team in January 1999 at the age of just 18, and proved an immediate hit, scoring three goals in his first two starts. He went on to play 11 games in the 1998–99 season, but failed to add any further goals to his opening gambit. During his first season in Sofia, he was joined in the first team by current Manchester City winger Martin Petrov and Aston Villa midfielder Stilian Petrov, who were also part of CSKA's youthful first team setup. However, Martin departed CSKA for Swiss outfit Servette in 1998 after only six months in the first team, and at the culmination of the 1998–99 season, Stilian headed to Scotland to play for Glasgow giants Celtic in the Scottish Premier League.

Despite juggling the demands of compulsory military service, which warranted a reduced, yet mandatory 18-month term after 1990, and the rigours of first team football with CSKA, Berbatov played and helped CSKA to win the Bulgarian Cup in 1999. A late goal secured a 1-0 win over the newly crowned league champions Litex Lovech – champions for a second season in succession – in the process denying the little club from the north of Bulgaria a first ever league and cup double. The victory also assured CSKA of qualification for the UEFA Cup for the 1999/00 season, after the club had only managed a disappointing fifth place finish in the Bulgarian first division.

The following season he cemented his place as a first team regular. With his reputation burgeoning and the scouts of a number of western clubs beginning to take notice of Bulgaria's hottest new talent, he impressed by scoring 14 league goals in 27 appearances for the first team, at an average of more than a goal every two games.

Yet, at the age of just 19, the teenager's popularity with the club's demanding supporters deteriorated drastically when, in May 2000, he squandered a number of chances to score the vital winning goal in a crucial title decider with arch-rivals Levski Sofia. Levski went on to win the game and, as a result the title, with CSKA's fans happy to vent their anger and frustration at their talented yet young and inexperienced striker. Nevertheless, despite his tender years, he proved he was man enough to take the flak being dished out by his detractors and shoulder the blame, when after the match he admitted: 'I am the culprit.'

During the summer, on the back of his first full season in the first team, Berbatov nearly packed his bags to head for the south-east of Italy and the newly-promoted Serie A club, Lecce, only to see the move fall through at the last minute. After a summer to get over the devastation of losing the title to their biggest rivals at the season's death, Berbatov returned to action determined to atone for his misses in that game. Unfortunately for him though, CSKA were unable to beat deposed champions Litex Lovech in their opening game of the new campaign, with the match ending scoreless.

Personal glory followed however as two goals in the UEFA Cup qualifying first leg victory over Constructorul of Moldova, followed by a sensational five-goal haul in the second leg, alerted the attention of Bundesliga giants Bayer Leverkusen and their manager Christoph Daum.

Shortly afterwards with the Bulgarian league season still in its infancy, CSKA announced that a deal had been agreed with the club from the Rhineland region of western Germany for the transfer of Berbatov. The move would go through on 1 January 2001, when the mid-season transfer window reopened. A number of his Bulgarian compatriots were already plying their trade in the Bundesliga, yet Berbatov's own transfer to Germany ensured he would set a small piece of history by becoming the first Bulgarian to play for Bayer 04 Leverkusen Football Club.

With forwards of the calibre of experienced internationals Oliver Neuville and Ulf Kirsten already on the Leverkusen payroll and established as the team's first choice forward partnership, Berbatov faced a gargantuan task to break up the duo upon his arrival in Germany. Never one to shy away from a challenge though, Berbatov, speaking with a maturity beyond his years, told *World Soccer* magazine:

'Leverkusen have many great forwards and there's sure to be huge competition for places. But I won't be overawed and will work as hard as I can to be a success there. I'm proud to have the chance to play for one of the best clubs in Germany. A lot of Bulgarians have gone to Germany and become better players. I hope to do the same.'

After CSKA's unscrupulous fans had blamed him for the club's elimination at the first round stage of the UEFA Cup at the hands of MTK of Hungary, Berbatov responded in defiant fashion by rattling home nine goals in 11 games in his last few months at the club, to silence his vocal critics. He departed the Bulgarian Army Stadium, CSKA's home turf, for the princely sum of around £1.5 million, leaving his team-mates in good shape to challenge for the league championship. During his two-and-a-half seasons at CSKA Dimitar notched an impressive strike rate of 26 goals in 49 games.

With a series of physical attacks on a number of high profile figures within the sport in Bulgaria, the timing of the transfer appeared perfect for one of the country's brightest hopes. A new and exciting chapter in Berbatov's fledgling career lay in wait as the young forward departed the volatile world of Bulgarian football for pastures new and a future playing alongside seasoned internationals including Michael Ballack, Bernd Schneider and the Brazilians Lucio and Ze Roberto.

When Berbatov had signed for Leverkusen, he had done so under the impression that he would be working under the vastly experienced coach, Christoph Daum. But prior to his arrival at his new club in January 2001, a situation occurred which tainted the club's friendly image and prevented him from having the chance to work with the man who had taken Leverkusen to three Bundesliga runners-up finishes in the past four seasons.

Daum had parted company with the club in October 2000 after failing a dope test. He had been scheduled to replace Germany's caretaker coach Rudi Voller as the new coach of the *Nationalmannschaft* at the end of the league season. Instead, the job offer was rescinded by the German Federation (DFB) and Leverkusen dispensed with his services. Rudi Voller, Leverkusen's sporting director, in addition to his role as caretaker coach of

Germany, briefly took over first team affairs at the club before former national manager Berti 'The Terrier' Vogts stepped in to take the reins as the new head coach in November. He had never managed a club side before his appointment into the Leverkusen hot seat, but his record of 67 wins from 102 internationals with only 12 defeats during his time in charge of the national team clearly indicated his ability to get results on the biggest stage.

With Leverkusen challenging near the top of the table upon his arrival, Vogts was keen to voice his aims for the remainder of the season to his many critics: 'I can only hope to build on the good foundations laid by Daum and Voller. All is in place for us to achieve our dual goal of qualifying for Europe and playing wholehearted, entertaining and winning football.'

And his reign got off to the best possible start with comfortable Bundesliga victories in his first two matches in charge over Hamburg and Kaiserslautern. However, Vogts' ambitions of success in Europe evaporated with the club's elimination from the Champions League in the first group phase. Subsequently the club would have to play AEK Athens of Greece in the UEFA Cup second round. A thrill-a-minute 4-4 draw at the BayArena precluded a disappointing 2-0 defeat in Athens, thus ending the club's hopes of European success for another season. Following a further three away defeats in the Bundesliga in December, Berbatov arrived in Germany with his new club occupying fourth place in the table, just three points behind leaders Schalke, and still in a decent position to challenge for a first ever Bundesliga championship win.

Nevertheless, Berbatov faced a fight to get a game for

the first team from the outset. Upon his arrival, Vogts had inherited the luxury of a squad and forward line packed with experience and international caps. In addition to the aforementioned presence of Kirsten and Neuville, Berbatov also had to contend with competition from the Brazilian-born German international Paulo Rink, Thomas Brdaric and the highly-rated American teenager Landon Donovan. Winning a first team place was never going to be instantaneous and the young Bulgarian, as it proved, would have to bide his time and wait for his opportunity.

Ulrich Dost, the press officer for Leverkusen, admitted the teenager was a touch reserved and apprehensive upon his arrival in Germany, with the customs adopted within the squad proving somewhat alien to what he had been accustomed back in home in Bulgaria.

'When he joined Leverkusen he really was very shy' Dost said. 'For example, he wasn't used to the custom among the players and staff of shaking hands every morning. Early on, it became clear that he was very much his own man. He was, however, given every support by his team-mates and the club in general. He communicated more by look rather than words. His parents stayed in Bulgaria. His father visited him from time to time. And he flew back home whenever he could.'

With his family remaining at home in Bulgaria, Berbatov faced a tough battle to settle into a foreign country with a foreign language and an alien culture. Dost continued: 'He didn't speak a word of German. But he already spoke very good English. He was quick to learn German but he tended not to be very talkative.'

Upon the resumption of league action after the mid-season break, Leverkusen's inconsistent form continued as two defeats cost them the chance to lead the table going into March. Yet, with their closest rivals dropping crucial points in March, Leverkusen cemented their title credentials with a vital 3-1 victory over Dortmund at the Westfalenstadion. However, the team's inconsistencies in April saw them fall back down to fourth place in the league with just four games of the season remaining. And, a dramatic late defeat at the BayArena to Bayern Munich effectively ended the Rhineland club's title ambitions, as they were forced to settle for a fourth place finish.

Once again the team had promised so much, yet delivered so little. Berbatov had figured on six occasions in his first half-season at the club, but his chances of figuring more prominently the next season were significantly boosted when veteran striker Kirsten, announced that the 2001–02 season would be his last as a professional footballer. As for Vogts, whose tenure had yielded a disappointing nine league defeats, his short reign in charge was brought to a clinical conclusion when the club's hierarchy fired him within 24 hours of the season's closure.

The club was in desperate need of a motivator; somebody who could get the best out of the talented players at his disposal, inspire them to realise their undoubted potential and ultimately put together a stronger and longer-lasting challenge for honours.

CHAPTER 3

TREBLE TROUBLE

'If you are first you are first. If you are second you are nothing.'
FORMER LIVERPOOL MANAGER, BILL SHANKLY

The 2001–02 campaign proved to be a truly remarkable one for Dimitar Berbatov and everybody associated with Bayer 04 Leverkusen Football Club. Nevertheless, it also proved to be one of the most frustrating and heartbreaking campaigns that the club and its relatively small army of devoted fans had ever experienced.

Following a turbulent season which had seen head coach Christoph Daum depart the club in ignominy and embarrassment after failing a doping test, and his successor Berti Vogts dismissed on the back of an ultimately disappointing seven-month tenure, Leverkusen announced on 1 July 2001 the appointment of ex-Eintracht Frankfurt and Bochum coach, Klaus 'Toppi' Toppmoller, who would assume overall control of team affairs.

Vogts' main flaw during his short stint in charge had been his inability to win the backing of the club's fans and sustain the club's title challenge as the season drew to a conclusion. The team had only just managed to scrape a fourth place finish – to at least ensure Champions League qualification once again – despite leading the Bundesliga at one stage.

Toppmoller had inherited a squad bristling with international talent, but immediately set about recruiting new players to deal with the challenging rigours of domestic and European competition. In came the penalty-taking German international goalkeeper Hans-Jorg Butt on a free transfer from former European champions Hamburg, and the talented Turkish international schemer, Yildiray Basturk from Bochum.

Toppmoller outlined his aims in *World Soccer* magazine ahead of the forthcoming season, highlighting in particular that his relationship with the players would be a much closer one than they had previously enjoyed under Vogts' stewardship. He said: 'What's gone has gone. There is a new team spirit here. The boys are highly motivated to do well in both the Bundesliga and Europe. Not one so-called expert thinks we are going to have a good season, and it rankles. We want to show we are still alive. I dismissed the sports scientist employed by predecessor [Berti Vogts]. The trust between the players and the coach is fundamental. No one should come between us.'

After making just six appearances in his first half-season at Leverkusen, Berbatov went into the 2001–02 campaign looking to establish himself as a first team regular under the new coach. His hopes of realising such ambitions had already received a significance boost with 35-year-old veteran striker Ulf Kirsten's admission that the season would be his last. Unfortunately for the Bulgarian rookie though, his hopes of impressing Toppmoller were temporarily dashed early on, when he and fellow forward Paulo Rink suffered knee injuries that would rule them both out of contention for a first team place at the start of the season.

Toppmoller's team began the season confidently, recording victories in their opening two Bundesliga matches and were only denied a morale-boosting early season victory over perennial title challengers, Bayern Munich, when Giovane Elber's late equaliser cancelled out Kirsten's opener at the BayArena. After the opening three matches of the season, Leverkusen occupied third place in the table, two points behind a Borussia Dortmund team inspired by the goals of their new multi-million pound signing from Parma, Marcio Amoruso, and second-placed Kaiserslautern.

A thrill-a-minute match against local rivals Schalke finished dramatically as Leverkusen snatched a point from the jaws of defeat when a late goal from midfielder Bernd Schneider clinched a 3-3 draw. Meanwhile, qualification for the group stages of the Champions League was assured late in August thanks to a 3-0 victory over 1991 European Champions Red Star Belgrade at the BayArena, before the fit-again Berbatov and his international colleagues headed off to represent their countries in the on-going World Cup qualifiers.

Berbatov helped himself to a brace of goals as his

country kept alive their qualification hopes with a 2-0 victory in Malta. And with their closest Group 3 rivals Denmark and Czech Republic dropping points the same day, the young striker and his team-mates finished the day at the top of the group standings. But, a devastating 2-0 reverse inflicted in Sofia by the Danes meant Berbatov and his countrymen faced the difficult proposition of defeating the Czech Republic in their own backyard to retain a chance of qualifying for the tournament to be held in South Korea and Japan.

Further victories back in the league in the meantime enhanced Leverkusen's title challenge, before a superb 1-0 away win over Olympique Lyon of France got the club off to an excellent start in the Champions League group stages. A huge top-of-the-table derby clash against Dortmund – who themselves had secured a battling 0-0 draw against Liverpool in the week – at the Westfalenstadion awaited Leverkusen on their return to league action.

Looking to show off their title credentials, Leverkusen spent the majority of the match on the back foot after the *Dortmunder* took an early lead through the free-scoring Brazilian Amoruso. But despite dominating the match from start to finish, Dortmund were unable to muster a second goal to kill off their opponents as Leverkusen battled to find a priceless equaliser.

And the day proved a momentous one in the career of Berbatov when, with 10 minutes of the match remaining, he latched on to a left wing cross to tap home the easiest of chances from close range and rescue a point – his first ever league goal in the black and red kit of Leverkusen.

However, despite scoring his first goal for the club, Berbatov still faced a mammoth task to secure a starting berth ahead of Kirsten and Neuville who had both started the season in the goals.

After watching Berbatov level a match that the home team should really have won, Dortmund coach Matthias Sammer – the former German midfield maestro – revealed his frustration with his team's inability to finish off a dogged Leverkusen side: 'At half-time, we would not have been flattered by a 3-0 or even a 5-0 lead. If we are to be a big team, we have to have more of a killer instinct.'

Three days later, Leverkusen welcomed 1992 European champions Barcelona to the BayArena, but despite the Catalan side boasting a star-studded lineup, Toppmoller's men were not overawed as they came from behind to record a wonderful 2-1 victory over the Spanish giants, to keep their 100 per cent record in the 2001–02 Champions League intact. Leverkusen also finished September in third position in the Bundesliga table – the only team still to have not lost a league game – and with only three points separating them from Kaiserslautern and Bayern Munich in first and second spots.

A delighted Toppmoller – still in the early days of his Leverkusen reign – hailed his team's spirit and hard-working performances, after a highly satisfactory month, saying: 'What has really pleased me is the absolute will to win and unbelievable team spirit that has developed here. The mindset of the lads has become so much stronger. We believe in ourselves.'

Meanwhile, Berbatov and his Bulgarian compatriots

saw their dreams of qualifying for the 2002 World Cup finals go up in smoke in early October. With nothing less than victory an absolute necessity, Bulgaria were humiliated 6-0 by a rampant Czech side in Prague, culminating in the resignation of head coach, Stoicho Mladenov. Berbatov began the game on the bench, only entering the fray after 20 minutes with his team already trailing by two goals. Unfortunately, the game was already over as a contest by the time of Berbatov's arrival, as was any hope of qualification, and the Czechs rubbed salt in the wounds of the visitors scoring a further four goals.

The Champions League provided a welcome tonic for Berbatov though when, with a quarter of the group game against Fenerbahce remaining, Toppmoller gave him his European debut in a Leverkusen shirt in place of Olivier Neuville. 'Berbo' – as he had become known to his new team-mates and friends in Germany – helped his team to a 2-1 win and, in the process, the brink of qualification for the second group phase of the competition.

Berbatov showed his striking prowess two weeks later when he was on the spot to turn home a cross at the back post from the Croatian defender Boris Zivkovic and wrap up an emphatic 4-1 home win over VFB Stuttgart. Then, despite succumbing to defeat at the Camp Nou to Barcelona, Leverkusen bounced back to record a hard-fought win over Fenerbahce in Turkey to seal progression to the second group stage of the Champions League with a game to spare.

With one match in Group F remaining – the dead-rubber against Lyon – Toppmoller decided to give

Berbatov his chance up front with Neuville and Kirsten both rested. Despite losing the match 4-2, Berbatov rewarded Toppmoller's faith in him by displaying his excellent range of skills and outstanding ability to score a wonderful solo goal in the defeat.

With the race for the title beginning to gather pace, Leverkusen remained hot on the heels of leaders Bayern Munich at the start of November – after an impressive run of four league victories including a 2-1 win over title rivals Kaiserslautern thanks to a brace of goals from Michael Ballack. But with Bayern dropping valuable points throughout November and Toppmoller's men extending their winning sequence, it was Leverkusen who topped the first table of December, despite stumbling at the start of the month to their first defeat of the season, away at Werder Bremen. A heavy 4-0 defeat away at two-time European champions Juventus saw the resumption of Champions League duty begin disappointingly, but a comfortable 3-0 home win over Deportivo La Coruna the following week put the club back in contention to qualify out of a group also containing English giants Arsenal.

Leverkusen entered into the mid-season winter break as autumn champions for the first time in their history – level on points with a resurgent Dortmund but ahead on goal difference – despite losing a further two games before Christmas. Bayern Munich also wobbled as they managed only two points from a possible nine. Toppmoller pointed to the loss of key players, including Lucio, Michael Ballack, Bernd Schneider, and skipper Jens Nowotny to injury as the reason for their pre-Christmas slump. He admitted to the German press: 'We simply lack the quality in depth and can't make up when these key players aren't there.' Leverkusen also received a major pre-Christmas blow, when it was revealed that Bayern had agreed a deal to sign Toppmoller's midfield general, Ballack, at the season's end in a multi-million pound deal.

When the Bundesliga restarted late in January after the winter break, Leverkusen kicked off proceedings with a home win over Hansa Rostock. Meanwhile, Bayern slumped to an emphatic 5-1 defeat at the hands of Schalke in Gelsenkirchen, not the ideal preparation for their forthcoming heavyweight clash with Leverkusen at the Olympiastadion in Munich. Nevertheless, despite their recent woes, Bayern lifted themselves for the match and goals from Elber and a Stefan Effenberg penalty clinched the three points for the Bavarians. Another disappointing defeat the following weekend and their first of the season at the BayArena, this time to arch-rivals Schalke, allowed Dortmund to open a four-point gap over Leverkusen at the top of the table.

Once again though, Leverkusen's mental strength came to the fore in February as they bounced back to rein in Dortmund's lead at the top of the table. A 5-0 thrashing of Borussia Monchengladbach – Berbatov grabbing the fifth of a dominant performance – got the Rhinelanders back on track, while Bayern and Dortmund shared a 1-1 draw at Bayern's Olympiastadion.

Two weeks later Leverkusen welcomed Dortmund to the BayArena. Yet, what had been billed as Dortmund's day to confirm their status as title favourites, steadily turned into a nightmare for the Ruhr valley club. A feisty match with plenty of bite saw Leverkusen open the scoring 30 minutes in when Ballack side footed home. The lead doubled early in the second half when Carsten Ramelow headed home from close range after Jens Lehmann – in the Dortmund goal – contrived to gift him the simplest of opportunities. Neuville added a third before Berbatov, on as a substitute yet again, stroked home another late goal and Leverkusen's fourth to seal an emphatic victory and top spot in the league.

After the final whistle Ballack told the press of the significance of the victory for Leverkusen – and their other rivals' – in the race for the title: 'Returning to the top of the table is very encouraging. This result will go down very well with the other teams in contention.'

Leverkusen dropped two further points the following week as they drew away at Freiburg but a draw for Dortmund ensured Toppmoller's side remained at the summit of the league as March kicked in. Progression to the knock out stages of Europe's most prestigious and lucrative tournament, though, would prove tough after a draw and defeat to Arsenal in the Champions League left Leverkusen languishing at the foot of their group and in need of two victories from their remaining two matches to progress.

The month of March proved an extremely rewarding one for Leverkusen after the draw with Freiburg, as the team notched four consecutive victories to increase their lead at the top of the Bundesliga to four points with only five matches left to play. The team also produced two fantastic performances against the *Old Lady* – Juventus – and Deportivo La Coruna to progress at the expense of the Italians and Arsenal to the quarter-final stage of the Champions League.

It was also a month to remember for Berbatov, who enjoyed a starting role in the crucial group win over Juventus, and also took his goals tally in the league to a respectable seven for the season – in the process helping the team to some must-win results. First he scored yet another late goal against Energie Cottbus to seal a 2-0 win before adding a vital second with a controlled volley in the 2-0 triumph over Stuttgart. An emphatic 4-0 destruction of 1860 Munich preceded a late victory away at Kaiserslautern, as Leverkusen scored twice in the last 13 minutes to settle a game they looked to have thrown away having led 2-0 at one point, Berbatov notching his now almost mandatory late goal to seal maximum points for the club.

With a huge Champions League last-eight tie against Liverpool awaiting them, a four-point lead over Dortmund with five matches remaining in the Bundesliga, and a German Cup Final against holders Schalke to look forward to in May – after a 3-1 extra-time win over arch-Rhineland rivals Cologne 3-1 in the semi-finals – Leverkusen entered the business-end of the season confident of rewarding their passionate fans with some long overdue silverware.

April began with a trip to the north-west of England and Anfield to face UEFA Cup holders and four-time European champions Liverpool in the Champions League. Liverpool skipper Sami Hyypia turned home a Michael Owen centre just seconds before the half-time whistle to give the Merseyside team the lead, but the

Leverkusener held out to take just a one-goal deficit home and into the second leg the following week.

The team warmed up for the vital second leg with a comfortable 2-0 victory over local rivals Cologne, while title rivals Bayern Munich lost further ground on them when they conceded a last minute equaliser to Werder Bremen in Munich. Dortmund remained in touch with Leverkusen, meanwhile, when they defeated Munich's other team, 1860, the following day.

Liverpool arrived in Germany as the firm favourites to qualify for the semi-finals and a potential showdown with bitter rivals Manchester United, courtesy of their first leg lead and big match pedigree in the competition. Nevertheless, Leverkusen were determined not to be overawed by the occasion and proceeded to take the game to their more illustrious opponents from the first blast of the referee's whistle. It would prove to be a seesaw battle of epic proportions and one of the greatest Champions League games ever witnessed.

Leverkusen, who adopted a highly offensive strategy under Toppmoller's orders, were rewarded when a stunning piledriver from the left foot of Ballack flew into the top corner of the Liverpool goal to give the team the perfect start just 15 minutes into the game. But, just three minutes before half-time, Liverpool's Portuguese international defender, Abel Xavier, was allowed to rise unchallenged to head home a Danny Murphy corner. The away goal now meant that Toppmoller's men had to win by two clear goals to win through the tie.

During the half-time break, Toppmoller made a decisive and ultimately match-changing decision. Off came the veteran Kirsten and Zoltan Sebescen, a midfielder, and on came Neuville – who had started the match on the bench – and more intriguingly Berbatov, to add an extra attacking dimension to the Leverkusen lineup. Having scored a number of important goals from the bench already that season, Toppmoller obviously felt the Bulgarian striker could provide the spark to get Leverkusen back in the match. Yet, it was Liverpool who appeared destined to wrap up the match, only for the normally deadly Owen to twice squander clear-cut one-on-one chances with Butt in the Leverkusen goal.

Having been let off the hook by England and Liverpool's star striker, Leverkusen continued to attack and gave themselves a chance when Ballack headed home to bring the aggregate scores level. However, Liverpool remained in front by virtue of their superior away goals count. Leverkusen were still in need of another goal to qualify at Liverpool's expense.

As the team poured forward in search of a vital third, Neuville had a goal-bound shot blocked on the line by Liverpool defender Stephane Henchoz. The ball rebounded to Berbatov who displayed calmness personified to poke home, causing his coach Toppmoller to dance excitedly on the touchline, as Leverkusen took the lead on aggregate 3-2. But any thoughts that the match was over were shattered once again when Finnish forward Jari Litmanen – on as a first half replacement – tiptoed his way through the Leverkusen defence to fire a precise shot into the corner of the net to put Liverpool back in front courtesy of the away goals rule for the second time in the match.

With only 10 minutes of the match remaining when the Finn scored Liverpool's second of the night, it looked a tall order for the German side to haul themselves off the deck for a third time. But, with just over five minutes of the 90 remaining, the Brazilian defender Lucio abandoned his defensive responsibilities to add further weight to the Leverkusen attack. And his gamble paid instant dividends when he hammered home a left-footed winner from Yildiray Basturk's defence-splitting pass, to send the home crowd wild with delight and Toppmoller's men through to the semi-finals in a shock result.

Four years later in a Tottenham match day programme, Berbatov revealed how that incredible game held special memories for him: 'It was maybe one of the greatest games I have played in up to now – it was unbelievable. We lost 1-0 at Anfield. Then at home there was everything you want to see in a game. Goals, great play and I scored! It was an evening I will not forget and a memory I treasure.'

After the euphoria of the unexpected victory over Liverpool, Leverkusen returned to league action and their title challenge with a trip to the north of Germany and a fixture with Hamburg. An early goal from Sergei Barbarez was quickly cancelled out by Neuville's strike, but Leverkusen were unable to find a winning goal which gave Bayern Munich and Dortmund an opportunity to gain ground on them in the table. Bayern managed a win over Nurnberg but Dortmund succumbed to defeat at the hands of Kaiserslautern the following day to leave Leverkusen still holding a four-point lead with just three matches to play. Surely they wouldn't slip up again, as they had in years gone by, would they?

Their four-point lead evaporated into a single point advantage after the very next game as Leverkusen finally lost their unbeaten home record at the worst possible time with a 2-1 defeat at the hands of Werder Bremen. Meanwhile, a last minute penalty for Dortmund, despatched by Amoruso, gave them a crucial 2-1 win at home to Cologne while Bayern Munich retained their own slight title aspirations with a 3-0 home win over Hertha Berlin. What had appeared an infallible lead now looked decidedly fragile as Leverkusen's attentions were once again drawn away from the title race to the Champions League and a semi-final clash at Manchester United's Old Trafford stadium.

Having impressed Toppmoller with another goalscoring cameo as a substitute in the unexpected defeat of Liverpool, Berbatov found himself named in the starting lineup for the decisive away leg at United's Theatre of Dreams. Yet, despite twice going behind in the match to goals from Ole Gunnar Solskjaer and a penalty from the lethal Ruud van Nistelrooy, Leverkusen were determined to take advantage of their best opportunity to reach a first-ever Champions League final. Firstly, Ballack netted to bring the scores equal at 1-1 before Neuville, on as a replacement for Berbatov, struck a priceless equaliser within three minutes of his introduction to give Leverkusen a draw and a vital second away goal to take into the return leg to be played at the BayArena a week later.

The pressure of battling on three fronts for silverware was beginning to show as Leverkusen slumped to yet another crushing defeat with a devastating 1-0 away reverse at the hands of Nurnberg. They had now surrendered what had been a five-point lead only two games before to allow Dortmund to take pole position in the race for the Bundesliga title. The repercussions of the defeat for Leverkusen meant they would have to win their final game at home to Hertha Berlin and pray that Werder Bremen could take at the very least, a point from their game away at Dortmund if the Bundesliga title was to make its way to the BayArena for the first time in the club's history.

After the setback suffered at the hands of Nurnberg in their penultimate Bundesliga match of the season, Leverkusen returned to Champions League duty and entered the second leg of the semi-final with Manchester United determined to make amends for the stuttering end to their season that looked likely to cost them a maiden championship win. Despite falling behind to Roy Keane's early opener for United, a goal on the stroke of half-time from Neuville ensured Leverkusen held on to go through to the final – to be held at Glasgow's Hampden Park – on the away goals rule.

The victory also meant Leverkusen would be the first team ever to reach the final of the competition having not won their domestic league the previous season. Now, only Real Madrid – who had knocked out fierce rivals Barcelona in the semi-finals – stood between Leverkusen and a second European trophy to add to the UEFA Cup they had won back in 1988.

Four days after despatching the challenge of English champions United, Leverkusen welcomed Hertha Berlin to the BayArena for the final league game of the season.

Two goals from Michael Ballack – playing his final league game for the club before his departure to title rivals Bayern – ensured a winning end to the season for the club. Meanwhile, across at nearby Dortmund, Paul Stalteri (who some years later in his career would turn out alongside Berbatov) had given Werder Bremen the lead in their clash and the unthinkable was on. If Bremen could hold out for a win or at least a draw, the title would go to Leverkusen. But an equaliser from the giant Czech striker Jan Koller meant Dortmund only needed one more goal to secure the Bundesliga title for a third time in their history.

With just 16 minutes of the match remaining and with the score all square at 1-1, it looked as though Leverkusen's hopes of clinching the title were steadily improving all the time. A draw between the teams would mean a long-awaited piece of silverware for Leverkusen and a first winners' medal for Berbatov in the black and red kit since his arrival in Germany. However, with only his second touch of the ball after entering the fray as a substitute, the Brazilian, Ewerthon, fired home to give Dortmund a 2-1 advantage. It spelt disaster for Leverkusen. Dortmund managed to hold out for victory and hence the title was theirs and not Leverkusen's.

There would be no Bundesliga winners' medal for Berbatov and his team-mates yet again. They had conspired to throw away a clear lead, and what had seemed unimaginable only a few weeks earlier had become a despairing reality once again. Despite defeating Hertha Berlin, they had finished second for the fourth time in six seasons, one point behind Dortmund and one ahead of Bayern Munich who had put together a run of four consecutive victories to go into the final game of the season with a faint chance of winning the title themselves.

After the realisation of having gifted the title to Dortmund had sunk in, Leverkusen's general manager Reiner Calmund blamed the team's league capitulation on player fatigue and the pressure of competing in three competitions. He told the press: 'After so many games at home and abroad, we were not fresh enough in the last few weeks of the season. We had become tired and lacked the necessary aggression in our game. Luck was not with us either. Until the closing stages we'd had a great season. It's very difficult to accept, and some of the players are in tears. All the same, congratulations to Dortmund. If you are top at the end of 34 rounds, you are worthy champions.'

Despite the fact that their title credentials had been questioned after they had failed to beat any of the other top teams including Leverkusen, Bayern and Schalke, Dortmund coach Matthias Sammer remained adamant that his team were worthy champions: 'No question – we deserved the title. We finished on top, and that's all there is to it. It's all very satisfying, and the team has to be complimented.'

A week after the anti-climactic end to their league campaign, Leverkusen had the opportunity to partially erase their disappointment when they travelled to the German capital, Berlin, to face Schalke in the final of the German Cup. Schalke had themselves suffered the ignominy of throwing away what had seemed a certain league title the previous season when Bayern Munich scored a late winner on the last day to cruelly deny them their own first-ever Bundesliga crown.

In front of a 70,000-strong crowd at the Olympiastadion, Berbatov gave Leverkusen's travelling support reason to believe that it would be their day, when he redirected a pass inside the near post for the first goal of the final. However, with just seconds of the first half remaining, Leverkusen conceded a free-kick within shooting range and Schalke's Jorg Bohme punished them to the maximum with a precise curling finish to send the sides in at half-time all square.

After the restart, Leverkusen appeared to be suffering the after-effects of Schalke's late first half equaliser as they struggled to settle back into the contest. Missed chances by Berbatov ensured the game remained all square before goals from Victor Agali, Andreas Moller and the Dane, Ebbe Sand gave Schalke an unassailable 4-1 lead. And despite conceding a last minute consolation to Ulf Kirsten, it was the team from the Ruhr that travelled home with the cup and the glory. After the defeat, Leverkusen's dejected German international midfielder Carsten Ramelow summed up the mood in the camp: 'What does it matter, 1-2, 1-3, we didn't play well. With our marking, you couldn't win.'

Having squandered the league from what had seemed an unassailable position, and after losing the domestic cup final, too, Leverkusen were heartlessly labelled 'Neverkusen' once again by the German press in jest at the team's inability to finish the job. Now, Leverkusen faced the toughest task of all if they wanted to end the season with a trophy to show for their incredible efforts, and silence their critics.

Real Madrid – eight times winners of the European Cup since its inception in 1955 – who had assumed the nickname *Los Galacticos* from the Spanish press for their president Florentino Perez's penchant for purchasing massively expensive superstar players of the reputation of Zinedine Zidane, Roberto Carlos and Luis Figo to add to homegrown stars such as Raul, would have to be overcome if Leverkusen were to become only the fourth German club to win the European Cup. Bayern Munich had already won the trophy four times in their history while fellow Bundesliga clubs, Hamburg and Borussia Dortmund had reached the pinnacle of club football on one occasion each. Could Leverkusen add their name to the list? Could Berbatov win the biggest prize of all? Would he get the opportunity to play?

Ahead of the biggest match in Leverkusen's history, Calmund was determined to look ahead with positive enthusiasm rather than dwell upon the disappointments of the previous two devastating weeks. He said in *The Independent*: 'In football only the present and the future matter and we have the biggest game in our history to look forward to. One billion fans will watch the match and I bet 800 million will be keeping their fingers crossed for us because we are David and Real Madrid are Goliath.'

Leverkusen were not the only ones who entered the game with something to prove however. Real had also failed to win the La Liga championship that season and had also lost in the Spanish Cup final at their own ground, the Bernabeu, much to the disgust of their fans. They were under enormous pressure, more so maybe than Leverkusen, to deliver a ninth European Cup to appease their trophy-hungry sponsors and supporters. And Toppmoller attempted to crank up the pressure on Real by telling the press: 'We're not the only ones with the same sort of problems. Real only came third in their championship and didn't win the Spanish Cup. But the Champions League Cup is the most important. We want to use all the qualities of discipline and strength to create problems for Real. I don't think we need motivation. We mean to show the world that we've got excellent players and an excellent team.'

Speaking ahead of his final game in Leverkusen colours before his summer transfer to Munich, goalscoring midfield dynamo Michael Ballack revealed to the press that the team remained undaunted by Real's European pedigree and pointed to the team's record of knocking out some of Europe's biggest club sides that season as a reason to be confident of victory. 'We would not have much of a chance if it were a two-legged final, but in the course of a single game we will be able to compensate for the loss of key players,' he said. 'We didn't make it to the final because we had easy draws. Does that not deserve some respect? We have only a small squad but whoever comes in is infected by the euphoria which surrounds us in European games.'

Before the final, Toppmoller spoke to the *Daily Mail* about his side's chances of ending the day victoriously, and in the process gaining revenge over Real, after they had beaten German side Eintracht Frankfurt 7-3 in the 1960 European Cup final. That game had also been staged at Hampden Park, and had been watched by Toppmoller as a child.

'It is my first memory of football and the first time I started dreaming about the sport,' he said. 'Any time a German team gets into a final, everybody in the country keeps their fingers crossed. I was hoping for Eintracht Frankfurt, then, even though all the big stars played for Real Madrid. But it does cross my mind now that, after 42 years, we might have some sort of revenge. Yes, maybe it is time for that. We'll see tomorrow night. I remember it so well, with Puskas getting four goals and Di Stefano three. It was an amazing time for Real Madrid. That victory, I think, was their fifth in a row in the European Cup. But, of course, they don't have Puskas and Di Stefano playing for them now.'

Meanwhile, Toppmoller was also keen to try and relieve some of the pressure on Ballack ahead of the biggest match of his career thus far. With the weight of expectation firmly fixed upon their star midfielder, Toppmoller admitted that Ballack should not be over-burdened and thought of as Leverkusen's only threat in the game: 'He can only play as well as the team. Michael has had a wonderful season for us and might find more space than he did in Saturday's Cup Final. But, if anything is going to give us victory, it is our team spirit. We know Real's strengths, just as we know their weaknesses and, obviously, we hope to use that knowledge to our advantage.

'They've got a lot of good players, 11 if I'm not mistaken. Maybe McManaman isn't quite of Figo's calibre. I feel very happy and comfortable. I'm really looking forward to what is the absolute highlight for us. I think we can look forward to a good game. I think there will be a few goals in it because I expect Real to play quite an attacking game. They, of course, are the great favourites to win. We, at least, can celebrate the game of football.'

With key defender Jens Nowotny already ruled out through injury and the Brazilian wide man Ze Roberto absent due to suspension, Leverkusen faced an enormous battle to prevent their season ending without a trophy to show for their efforts. However, Toppmoller was remaining upbeat about their chances of causing an upset, saying: 'We have overcome all sorts of difficulties already in this tournament. We have worked hard, also, to get where we are and I'm sure we will play with enthusiasm and all the other German qualities. We will be a strong, united team.'

And goalkeeper Hans-Jorg Butt and midfielder Carsten Ramelow showed their unity behind the coach, with Butt noting: 'We're not exactly favourites against Real but we aren't without optimism because we've beaten some great teams already.'

Ramelow, Leverkusen's acting captain for the night, echoed his team-mate's optimism, adding: 'I have played against Real Madrid several times and know how strong they are. Yet we are strong, also. We have nothing to fear.'

Meanwhile, there was little attention being placed on Berbatov, who had been named as a substitute for the match. But his international colleague Stilian Petrov, who was now plying his trade in Glasgow for Celtic, had no doubt that should Toppmoller call upon his young striker at any time during the game, Berbatov would be ready and able to answer the call with aplomb. Petrov told the *Glasgow Evening Times*:

'We both came through the youth ranks together and broke into the first team at CSKA Sofia at around the same time. We also played at youth level for Bulgaria together and became good friends. I knew he also wanted to move to a bigger club and further his career. So when he signed for Bayer Leverkusen I was delighted for him. Dimitar told me that he knew it was going to be very difficult to get a game there but he was so keen to do well.

'He was asking me about Hampden Park since I have played there a few times for Celtic, and I told him what to expect. The pitch has just been re-laid and I also told him that the supporters behind the goal are quite far away from the pitch. It isn't like a lot of stadiums where they can almost touch you. I'm not sure if this will help him or not, but you are better knowing as much as possible, especially in a game as big as this one.'

He continued: 'Dimitar is a goal scorer. He has always been good at putting the ball in the back of the net. It doesn't matter what level he is playing at or who he is playing against, he believes he can score and often that is indeed the case. I think he has improved a lot as a player since moving to Germany, the same as I have since I joined Celtic. No disrespect to our former clubs, because there are also a lot of good players there, but it helps to move on. And thankfully both of our moves seem to have worked out very well as I am winning things with Celtic and loving life in Scotland – and he is just one win away from winning the biggest prize in club football.'

When Real scored with their first real attack in only the ninth minute of the match, as Raul slotted home past Butt for the opening goal, it looked as though Leverkusen would be in for a torrid evening. But within the space of just five minutes, Leverkusen found themselves on level terms once again as giant Brazilian defender Lucio rose high above the static Madrid defence to head home the equaliser much to the delight of the travelling German fans within Hampden.

Calmed by the goal, the team settled into the match and began to attack Real's defence as they started to dictate the pace of the match. And, after going close through efforts from Brdaric and Zivkovic, Leverkusen were showing no signs of nerves on the biggest stage of all. Then, in the 38th minute, Toppmoller signalled for Berbatov to take off his tracksuit. This was his chance. He replaced the bemused Brdaric on the field but barely five minutes after coming on Leverkusen fell behind again this time to possibly the greatest goal ever scored in a Champions League Final. Latching onto a looping cross from the ever-dangerous Roberto Carlos, Zinedine Zidane swivelled to hit an unstoppable left-footed volley past the helpless Butt in Leverkusen's goal.

It was a goal worthy of winning such a game. But in the second half, Leverkusen to their credit kept coming forward, and when the referee signalled seven minutes of injury time, Toppmoller's men responded in positive fashion as they lay siege upon Madrid's goal. Firstly, in an attempt to cause confusion in the Madrid defence, Butt joined his team-mates in the area when Leverkusen won a free-kick in a dangerous area. And it was Butt who nearly made history when his header flashed narrowly past replacement goalkeeper, Iker Casillas' post. With time running out for Leverkusen to find a crucial equaliser to take the game into extra time, Casillas produced three stunning saves in quick succession to deny Basturk, Kirsten and Schneider certain goals. It wasn't to be for Berbatov and Leverkusen but they had every reason to be proud of themselves.

Speaking to the press after the final whistle, Toppmoller, who went on to be voted German Coach of the Year for 2002 despite missing out at the final hurdle in three competitions, said: 'We have come second again, but if someone had said we would be second in the Champions League when we started this, they would have thought it was mad. I am proud of what we have achieved this season, but we have played so hard and it hurts us to end with nothing.

'I think what we have achieved this season has been almost impossible given the problems we have had. The disappointment is huge – you don't always get the rewards you deserve in football, and no one knows that better than us after what we have been through. We must seek consolation. Doing what we have done means we have had a very good season – but what has happened to us is difficult and makes us feel bitter.'

And in the wake of further criticism at the team's failure to overcome the elusive final hurdle, Toppmoller told *World Soccer*: 'Those who say we choked don't know anything about football. Who got past Barcelona, Deportivo, Juventus, Arsenal, Liverpool and Manchester United? It was the "losers" from Leverkusen.'

Rainer Calmund meanwhile, admitted his pride at the team's achievements, telling *World Soccer*: 'In many ways this has been a wonderful season for us. I'm proud of the squad and coach Klaus Toppmoller, who has worked wonders for us since arriving last summer. However, it is also a harsh reality that when you don't win titles, you don't have nearly as much standing in today's world.'

As for Berbatov, despite missing out on three winners' medals, he had enjoyed a remarkable first full season in the Rhineland. His main objective now was to secure a regular starting berth in the first team and fire the club to trophies to make up for the disappointments of the 2001–02 season.

CHAPTER 4

LIFE ON THE RHINE

'He [Berbatov] was very popular with the fans as he scored so many goals.'
LEVERKUSEN PRESS OFFICER ULRICH DOST

After the massive disappointment of losing out at the final hurdle in three competitions the previous season, Leverkusen's hopes of going one better in the 2002–03 season were hardly boosted by the departures of Ballack and Brazilian team-mate and midfield partner Ze Roberto during the close season to Bundesliga rivals Bayern Munich. And, despite bringing in some highly-rated young talent and retaining the likes of defender Lucio, who had been strongly tipped to move to one of Italy's big clubs, Toppmoller faced a strict examination of his abilities to take the club close to the previous season's highs.

The squad was also dealt a massive blow when it was revealed that captain and key centre-back Jens Nowotny faced around eight months out with knee ligament damage. With Ulf Kirsten retiring from football at the end of the previous season it appeared to clear the path for Berbatov to stake a strong claim to become one of Toppmoller's first choice forwards. However, the signing of the Brazilian striker Franca from Sao Paulo ensured the competition for a starting berth remained high.

The season didn't get off to the best of starts for Toppmoller's new charges, as Leverkusen failed to win any of their opening three matches, losing 4-2 at home to newly-promoted Bochum and picking up only two points in the process. A 3-1 victory over Hansa Rostock gave the team their first three points of the season, but two defeats followed, the first a 3-1 reverse at home to Hannover, while the second, a 3-2 defeat away at Werder Bremen saw Berbatov pick up the only red card of his career to date just 12 minutes after coming on as a substitute, and also ruled him out of the following weekend's huge clash with Bayern Munich. The team also crashed badly in Europe, suffering a heavy 6-2 defeat away at Olympiakos before two goals from Ruud van Nistelrooy at the BayArena rendered Berbatov's first goal of the season mere consolation, as Manchester United gained a sense of retribution for losing out to Leverkusen in the semi-finals the previous season.

Without the suspended Berbatov, Leverkusen went into the match against Bayern as firm underdogs, the Bavarian team having strengthened considerably in the summer following their disappointing third place finish the previous season. However, a rasping free-kick from Lucio and a second half header from promising new recruit Daniel Bierofka gave Leverkusen a morale-boosting 2-1 win and denied Ballack and Ze Roberto victory on their first return to the BayArena. Toppmoller admitted his relief at the victory in *World Soccer*: 'I asked the boys to fight tooth and nail for the three points and that's what they did. We may have turned the corner. Despite losing at home to Manchester United in the Champions League, there were lots of positives in our display, and we improved still further against Bayern.'

Berbatov returned to the squad as a substitute for the vital midweek Champions League win over Maccabi Haifa in Cyprus to keep their hopes of qualification alive, but, despite the win over Bayern the club's inconsistent start to the league season continued with defeat away at Wolfsburg the very next weekend. A victory over Kaiserslautern and a draw away at Hertha Berlin improved the team's standing before yet another defeat, (their fifth of the season), this time at home to Stuttgart left the club languishing close to the bottom of the table and the relegation zone. One bright spot for the club however, came in the Champions League as two home victories over Maccabi and Olympiakos resurrected their chances of progressing out of their group.

Manchester United completed a double over Leverkusen at Old Trafford with a 2-0 win but the German side still progressed to the second group stage in second place after Maccabi and Olympiakos shared a 3-3 draw in the night's other match. Results in the Bundesliga didn't improve drastically in November either for Toppmoller's side as Berbatov's barren run without a goal continued and the team only managed one win and two draws and another home loss to Hamburg to end the month closer to the bottom of the table than the top.

The Bulgarian striker did manage another goal in the Champions League against Barcelona at the BayArena as the second group stage got underway, but the Catalan side recovered from a goal down to sneak a late 2-1 win and complete another miserable month for the Rhineland club.

December began with a satisfying 3-0 win over 1860 Munich on a freezing night in Bavaria as the club strove to turn the corner after a terrible run of form. Daniel Bierofka opened the scoring, before Berbatov finally grabbed his first Bundesliga goal of the season, sidefooting home Olivier Neuville's centre into a gaping net. Neuville completed the scoring with a carbon copy of Berbatov's goal, as Berbatov returned the favour with the killer pass. A 3-2 defeat away at Inter Milan in the Champions League left Leverkusen struggling to qualify out of their group for the knock out stages of the tournament. Then Nurnberg travelled to the BayArena for the final game before the mid-season winter break, as Leverkusen sought to gain revenge over the Bavarian club for virtually putting an end to their title challenge the previous season. However, history repeated itself as Nurnberg ran out 2-0 winners to leave struggling Leverkusen in a lowly 14th position, 19 points behind league leaders Bayern Munich and facing a fight to avoid relegation in the second half of the season.

Although the team finished 2002 in a sorry state, on a personal note the year finished on a high for Berbatov when he was named Bulgarian Player of the Year. Delighted at winning the award, he said: 'The first thing I did when I received the trophy was to hold it tight. This is the first I have won in my career. With Leverkusen, I touched the Champions League and the German Cup, but they eluded me. Now I hope my luck has changed.'

When the Bundesliga resumed in late January, Toppmoller's options were boosted by the welcome return of club captain Jens Nowotny after his recovery from knee ligament damage. However, in his very first game back, an embarrassing 3-0 home loss to Energie Cottbus, the unfortunate defender injured the same knee again, ruling him out indefinitely at a time when his experience would have proven invaluable. Toppmoller admitted his disappointment at Nowotny's breakdown and with the situation the team found themselves in, telling *World Soccer*: 'When things go wrong they really go wrong. Jens worked tremendously hard to get fit again and it's a severe blow to lose him for a second time. We must use Jens as an example. From now until the end of the season, the boys have to fight for him. Against Cottbus we could have played for two hours without scoring. We know we are right in the middle of a relegation struggle.'

A 2-0 defeat at Dortmund continued Leverkusen's dreadful form, although the team did manage to progress to the semi-finals of the German Cup by winning a penalty shoot-out against Unterhaching, to enhance their hopes of winning some silverware after the previous season's disappointments. But despite progress in the cup, Leverkusen's league form indicated the end was drawing near for Toppmoller, who had been unable to inspire the team to fight their way out of their slump. On the back of two further defeats at the start of February,

Reiner Calmund called time on 'Toppi's' short reign, saying: 'We are, of course, sorry to see Klaus go. He made us one of the best clubs in the world last season and his work was outstanding. But we're in a very precarious state and we had no choice.'

With the team struggling to alleviate the threat of relegation due to a lack of goals from Berbatov and his fellow strikers, and also a lack of clean sheets in defence, Leverkusen were linked with a number of possible replacements in the wake of Toppmoller's departure, as the rumour mill accelerated into overdrive. But in the end, the club's hierarchy settled on promotion from within, appointing Thomas Horster, a former Leverkusen player and coach with the youth and amateur sides, as Toppmoller's successor. The change in personnel appeared to do the team the world of good as they won their first two games under his leadership, significantly boosting their chances of remaining in the top division in the process.

However, a 3-1 defeat in the German Cup semi-finals to Bayern Munich, followed by back-to-back defeats to Newcastle United in the Champions League, ensured Leverkusen's last chance of a trophy evaporated and European participation ended prematurely for another season. Further defeats away at Barcelona and at home to Inter Milan condemned Leverkusen to a bottom place finish in their group without a point from six matches.

With the team lying perilously close to the relegation zone with only 10 league matches remaining, Horster could not have wished for a worse result than the 3-0 defeat inflicted by runaway leaders Bayern Munich in early March. Two late dropped points at the BayArena in the very next match against Wolfsburg and an away defeat against Kaiserslautern saw Berbatov and his team-mates staring down the barrel. The realisation of possible second division football the next season hit home with the team slumped in 17th position in the table.

An emphatic 4-1 victory over Hertha Berlin rekindled the team's hopes of retaining their top division status, but the following week a disheartening 3-0 defeat at Stuttgart dashed the fans' hopes that the team may have finally turned the corner. With the remaining matches beginning to run out, Leverkusen welcomed close neighbours Schalke to the BayArena for a crucial clash. The previous season, both clubs had been fighting it out near the top end of the table, but now, one year on, Leverkusen were fighting for their lives. And, with less than 10 minutes on the clock, Berbatov fired home for the home side to raise hopes of a vital victory. Unfortunately though, a wonder strike from Jorg Bohme and two further goals in the second half for Schalke subjected Leverkusen to yet another defeat, their 15th of a frustrating season to leave the club languishing.

With only five games of the season remaining, Leverkusen travelled to Monchengladbach in search of a crucial victory. Despite going a goal down early on in the game, Daniel Bierofka equalised in the first half before Berbatov, who had only scored two league goals all season, fired home just after the break to give Leverkusen a crucial lead. But the team's inability to defend came into evidence yet again as Monchengladbach forced home a last minute goal in the driving rain to deny Berbatov and the rest of the team some much-needed breathing space ahead of the following weekend's massive clash with fellow relegation candidates, Arminia Bielefeld.

Inspired by two goals from Lucio, Leverkusen overcame the challenge of Bielefeld 3-1 to boost the club's hopes of survival. But a 4-1 capitulation at the hands of Hamburg the following week continued the team's topsy turvy form as it became apparent to all concerned that the club's fight for survival would go down to the very last day of the season, no matter what the result of the penultimate match against 1860 Munich at the BayArena.

In the aftermath of the defeat to Hamburg, Horster strangely admitted to having given up hope of saving his charges from relegation, despite the fact that Leverkusen could retain their top division status if they could win their final two matches of the season. Horster, unsurprisingly some might say, was subsequently relieved of his duties, to be replaced by the legendary former Bayern Munich and West Germany defender, Klaus Augenthaler. The new man didn't exactly arrive with a glowing CV having recently being fired himself for failing to prevent Nurnberg from relegation. Would he accumulate the unwelcome statistic of taking two clubs down in one season? A 3-0 victory over the Bavarians of 1860 in Augenthaler's first match in charge ensured the club's destiny would go down to the final match of the season.

Bierofka opened the scoring against 1860 as he rifled the ball home from close range after being set up by good work from Berbatov. And the Bulgarian continued his recent good form by heading home the team's second just a minute before the half-time break to effectively seal the points for the *Leverkusener*. When Marko Babic added a third just minutes into the second half, it was clear for all to see the relief and joy on the faces of the players. The victory, coupled with defeat for Bielefeld at the hands of Hansa Rostock, ensured the club could now retain their Bundesliga status if they could avoid defeat away at already-relegated Nurnberg, Augenthaler's previous club.

And survival was indeed secured when Yildiray Basturk scored the winning goal in a 1-0 win over Nurnberg, while Bielefeld lost to a late goal at home to Hannover. In spite of one of the worst seasons in Leverkusen's history, survival had been guaranteed thanks to a late upturn in form and the players and fans celebrated joyously at the final whistle. Berbatov had played his part late in the season with some crucial goals but after two-and-a-half seasons in Germany, during which time he had still to make the kind of impact he would have wished for upon his arrival, the next season would need to be a good one for him. He had to prove to the club's hierarchy and fans that he could succeed at a big club playing in a tough division.

CHAPTER 5

GOALS, GOALS, GOALS

'Champions keep playing until they get it right.'
TENNIS LEGEND BILLIE JEAN KING

After narrowly avoiding the indignity of relegation to the German second division on the last day of the season in May, Leverkusen went into the 2003–04 season with Klaus Augenthaler confirmed as their permanent supremo following the departure of the 2001–02 German coach of the year, Klaus Toppmoller, and the ill-fated reign of Thomas Horster. However, despite their flirtations with the drop, Augenthaler failed to bring in the wave of expected high-profile new signings to strengthen a squad arguably lacking in depth. Only three relatively low-key signings were acquired, while Augenthaler trimmed the squad of fringe players he deemed to be surplus to requirements. Berbatov meanwhile traded in the number 12 shirt he had been allocated upon his arrival in Germany in January 2001, for the number nine shirt vacated by Ulf Kirsten upon his retirement and subsequent promotion to the club's coaching staff.

With only domestic competition to concentrate on for the first time since 1997, the lack of new personnel didn't appear to hinder the club early on as Augenthaler's Leverkusen impressed, winning their first three matches of the new campaign to head the early-season Bundesliga table, before succumbing to a first defeat of the season away at Bochum. However, the team managed to get back to winning ways immediately with a one-goal victory over Hamburg in preparation for their always highly-anticipated clash away at title favourites, Bayern Munich. And despite going behind three times to the Bavarian giants, with Michael Ballack scoring a thunderbolt against his former club, Leverkusen dug deep to secure a deserved 3-3 draw at the Olympiastadion.

The club finished September in second position in the league level on points with Werder Bremen and strengthened their position still further with a comfortable 3-0 win over Hansa Rostock. With the match scoreless at half-time, Berbatov entered the fray after 56 minutes and almost immediately helped create a rare goal for Argentine defender Diego Placente to break the deadlock. Then, just five minutes later, Berbatov, who had begun all eight previous league matches on the bench, opened his own account for the season. Latching onto a defence-splitting pass from playmaker Robson Ponte, Berbatov timed his run to perfection to break Rostock's offside trap before coolly rounding the advancing goalkeeper to double the team's advantage. And a fine solo effort from midfielder Daniel Bierofka put the gloss on a 3-0 win as Leverkusen's fine start to the new season under Augenthaler gathered pace.

After making a telling impact as a substitute in the win over Rostock, Augenthaler rewarded Berbatov with a starting role in the club's next match away at Hertha Berlin. And with the scores tied at 1-1, Berbatov repaid Augenthaler's faith in him when he lost his marker with a darting run to fire a smart finish into the top corner of the net to give Leverkusen the lead again. Two further goals wrapped up a stunning 4-1 victory for Leverkusen in the German capital to propel them to the top of the league standings.

A further four points from a possible six suggested the Rhineland club could silence the sceptics who doubted their ability to last the distance in the race for the championship. And it would have been a maximum six from six had Robson Ponte's shot not come back off the post in their match against Kaiserslautern after the Brazilian striker was put one-on-one with the goalkeeper following a delectable backheeled pass from Berbatov.

Berbatov took just three minutes of the club's next match against Schalke to put Leverkusen into the lead, as he toe-poked the ball over the advancing keeper, only to see his effort brilliantly thwarted on the line by a retreating defender. However, the defender's gallant efforts to prevent the goal proved in vain, when his attempted clearance fell directly back into Berbatov's path and the Bulgarian dispatched a left-footed shot into the roof of the net to open the scoring. Schalke struck back with the equaliser just 10 minutes later, but

Leverkusen wrapped up another impressive victory with further goals from Lucio and Bierofka.

A battling recovery away at Borussia Dortmund followed as the team fought back from 2-0 down to grab a point, before Leverkusen once again replicated a fighting spirit that had been notable by its absence the previous season, to again earn a share of the spoils after falling 2-0 behind at home to 1860 Munich. Augenthaler's bright start to his first full season in the Leverkusen hotseat saw the club finish November third in the league and just three points behind leaders Stuttgart.

A dour goalless draw away at arch-rivals Cologne followed by a 3-1 capitulation at the hands of new league leaders Werder Bremen cost Leverkusen the opportunity to add a second winter league title to the one they had won just two years previously. They did manage to bounce back, however, in their final game before the mid-season winter break when Berbatov provided the inspiration for a wonderful 3-2 away victory over fellow title challengers, Stuttgart. Leverkusen took a 2-0 lead into the interval courtesy of goals from experienced German international midfielder Carsten Ramelow, and a simple tap in on the stroke of half-time from Berbatov. Stuttgart narrowed the deficit early in the second half before Berbatov doubled his tally for the day with a sublime turn and curling shot to put Leverkusen comfortably into the driving seat, to render Stuttgart's second goal of the game mere consolation.

Berbatov, having gained the trust of Augenthaler following some impressive cameos from the bench, had begun to make a first team place his own, and with it he began to find the sort of scoring touch in the Bundesliga that had seen him become so prolific for the Bulgarian national team.

League action resumed in late January with Leverkusen occupying fourth position in the table. Berbatov volleyed a half-chance wide in the first half of a 1-0 defeat away at Freiburg, and the loss ensured any lingering doubts over the team's ability to sustain a season-long title challenge remained firmly intact. The team then contrived to lose even more ground on league leaders Werder Bremen and fellow title challengers Bayern Munich and Stuttgart with a home defeat at the hands of Eintracht Frankfurt. The visitors took the lead midway through the first half before a subtle header from Berbatov enabled Neuville to equalise with an hour played. But Leverkusen's poor start to the second half of the season continued when Frankfurt forced home a winner late on at the BayArena.

It looked as if the team's rotten run of form was destined to continue in the very next game when poor defending allowed Hannover to take a two goal lead in northern Germany. But Leverkusen – not for the first time in the season – fought back with a powerful close-range header from Berbatov and later sealed a point when the Brazilian forward Franca punished a defensive mix-up between goalkeeper and defender to fire home with a spectacular long-range strike.

After a less than inspiring start to 2004, Leverkusen welcomed Bochum to the BayArena as they sought to record a first victory of the new year. Yet, following a goalless first period Leverkusen found themselves two goals behind within 10 minutes of the second half kicking off. A pinpoint header from Berbatov on the hour from a free-kick reduced the deficit but a third goal from the away team inflicted a disappointing fifth defeat of the season upon the Rhineland club. And they followed it up with another 3-1 defeat at the hands of Hamburg as Leverkusen slipped down to fifth place in the league, a disappointing return given their promising start to the season.

March began as February had ended with another massively disappointing 3-1 defeat, this time at the hands of second placed Bayern Munich at the BayArena as Michael Ballack again notched a goal against his former employers. After a terrible run of form which had seen Leverkusen drop down to fifth in the table and in danger of fading out of contention for a place in Europe the next season, the team suddenly clicked to record a first win in seven matches as they played host to Wolfsburg the following weekend. Almost inevitably, it was Berbatov who opened the scoring with his seventh goal of the season, as he expertly turned his marker on the edge of the Wolfsburg penalty area and rammed home an unstoppable shot to give Leverkusen the perfect start with only one minute on the clock.

A delightful left-footed free-kick from Marko Babic doubled Leverkusen's advantage only for Wolfsburg to narrow the deficit with a goal of their own. However, Leverkusen restored their two-goal cushion before half-time as Berbatov again displayed his ability to set up as well as score goals, when he somehow managed to steer a difficult ball with his head into the path of Bernd

Schneider who was able to finish with consummate ease. Franca added a fourth after half-time and despite a second goal for Wolfsburg late on, Leverkusen finally put their terrible run of games without a win behind them.

Leverkusen travelled to the very north of Germany to face Hansa Rostock the next weekend in far more confident mood following the previous weekend's comfortable victory. Berbatov, who for the first time in his career at Leverkusen, was starting games and scoring goals on a regular basis, once again put Leverkusen on the road to victory as he lost his marker to latch onto a teasing cross from Schneider and put the ball past Rostock's helpless goalkeeper. And a precise volley later in the second half from Babic wrapped up a well deserved 2-0 victory for Leverkusen.

Hertha Berlin provided Leverkusen with their next opposition at the BayArena as Augenthaler's men sought to continue their impressive recent form. But when Brazilian free-kick specialist Marcelinho curled home an expertly taken dead ball, it looked as though Leverkusen's renaissance was about to come to an abrupt end. Unfortunately for the team from the capital though, Berbatov had begun to hit top form at exactly the right time for Leverkusen. And the Bulgarian international continued his impressive goalscoring streak when he found himself in acres of space to latch onto a long pass from Carsten Ramelow and hammer the ball home for the equaliser.

The in-form striker then turned provider when his strike partner Franca curled home a wonderful shot after getting on the end of Berbatov's flick on to give

Leverkusen a half-time lead. The Brazilian helped himself to a second soon after the break before Berbatov added to his own earlier strike, bamboozling his marker with sublime control and a fantastic turn in one movement before firing home. It capped a resounding victory which saw the club finish March in fourth position and back in serious contention for a place in the next season's Champions League.

After three successive victories, Borussia Monchengladbach ended Leverkusen's winning run as *The Foals* held their rivals from the Rhineland to a scoreless draw at Borussia-Park. But any thoughts that Leverkusen's challenge for a top three finish would be derailed by their failure to defeat their struggling neighbours were quickly diminished when they thrashed their south-Rhineland rivals Kaiserslautern 6-0 at the BayArena. Leverkusen took the lead in just the second minute when an inswinging corner from Schneider deflected into the net off the unfortunate *Red Devils* defender Timo Wenzel. Berbatov soon added a second when he reacted quickest to tap home from close range a mishit shot from Franca.

Star defender Lucio slid home a third following a fine burst forward and one-two with Berbatov, before Franca effectively ended the contest with a cool finish to put Leverkusen four goals to the good with only half the match played. Yildiray Basturk capped a fine passing move to curl home a fifth soon after the second half restart before Franca completed the rout with an acrobatic far post volley.

After completing their biggest win of the season,

Leverkusen faced a testing trip to close rivals Schalke in their next game as they aimed to step up the pressure on Stuttgart, the team currently occupying the final Champions League qualifying spot in third place. The blossoming forward partnership between Berbatov and Franca again bore fruit when the Brazilian played his Bulgarian colleague into a goalscoring position and Berbatov took full advantage to steer a classy finish with the outside of his foot past Schalke's helpless goalkeeper.

Schalke drew level early in the second half when the unfortunate Leverkusen skipper Jens Nowotny turned a cross shot into his own net. Schneider restored Leverkusen's advantage with a smart left footed shot before Berbatov found himself clear and with just Schalke's goalkeeper to beat, only to be brought down from behind by Jorg Bohme as he prepared to pull the trigger. The referee duly pointed to the spot and Leverkusen's penalty-taking goalkeeper Hans-Jorg Butt despatched the penalty with calm assurance. With Butt still retreating back to his area following his goal celebrations, Schalke proceeded to take a quick kick-off and striker Mike Hanke – aware that Butt was still some way off his line – spectacularly reduced the arrears with a remarkable chip from the halfway line. Despite Leverkusen's livid protestations the referee allowed the goal to stand but in the end the controversial decision proved irrelevant as Leverkusen held on for a vital victory in their quest for a third place Bundesliga finish.

Reigning champions Borussia Dortmund made the short journey to the BayArena on 1 May as Leverkusen sought to win a third game in a row with only five games of the season remaining. But the team from the Ruhr certainly didn't play like champions as they fell meekly to a 3-0 defeat. Babic coolly chipped goalkeeper Guillaume Warmuz for the opener before Berbatov carved open the static Dortmund defence for Turkish schemer Basturk to set up Franca for an easy second. Ten minutes after the half-time break, Leverkusen wrapped up another important win when Berbatov calmly stroked home his 14th goal of the season from the penalty spot.

Unfortunately for Augenthaler and his team, Stuttgart appeared to be in no mood to drop any points whatsoever as they recorded their fourth straight victory to consolidate their third position in the league five points ahead of Leverkusen with only four games remaining. A defensive mix up in their next game against 1860 Munich in Bavaria saw Leverkusen fall behind early on, but Schneider dragged the team level with a calm finish following good work from Berbatov. Meanwhile, there was good news for Augenthaler the next day when Stuttgart failed to take advantage of Leverkusen's slip up when they were held to a 1-1 draw at home by high-flying Bochum.

And the following weekend there was even more good news for Augenthaler when Leverkusen comfortably defeated their already relegated arch rivals Cologne 2-0, thanks to a stunning long range goal from midfielder Clemens Fritz and a lethal finish from Franca. The same day, Stuttgart fell to a 2-1 defeat at the hands of Hamburg as the gap between themselves and Leverkusen was cut to just two points with the league season approaching its climax. Meanwhile, down in Bavaria, runaway leaders Werder Bremen wrapped up the Bundesliga title with two games to spare as they comfortably beat nearest rivals Bayern Munich 3-1 in the Bavarians' own backyard.

With just two games of the domestic season remaining and just two points separating Stuttgart and Leverkusen in the race for the all important and financially rewarding third place finish, Leverkusen faced an awkward looking trip to north-west Germany to face newly-crowned Bundesliga champions Werder Bremen. Augenthaler's team went into the match aware that they would need at the very least to match Stuttgart's result against Bayern Munich in order to have a chance of snatching third place in the last match of the season. If Leverkusen could secure the result they needed, the calendar as luck would have it, paired the two teams against each other at the BayArena in a winner-takes-all game on the final day of the season.

Champions Bremen went into the match against Leverkusen expecting to celebrate their title triumph in style in front of their jubilant home fans at the Weserstadion. However, Leverkusen usurped the home side's party with three goals in the opening 21 minutes as they set about ensuring the race for the third place would go down to the wire. Berbatov calmly set up the opening goal for Franca before the prolific strike duo combined to set up Daniel Bierofka for a rasping second. Berbatov then saw his close-range shot brilliantly saved by Bremen number one Andreas Reinke, only for Franca to react quickest to turn home the rebound.

Bremen scored twice in quick succession after half-time

as they threatened a stirring comeback, but Franca ended any hopes the fans may have had of crowning their championship triumph with a victory when he evaded a last ditch tackle to complete his hat-trick and restore Leverkusen's two-goal advantage. Soon after, Berbatov increased the lead as he nonchalantly looped a header over Reinke before Olivier Neuville wrapped up an emphatic 6-2 victory with a stunning finish. Leverkusen ensured the race for third would go down to the final day following Stuttgart's impressive 3-1 win over Bundesliga runners up, Bayern Munich.

And so, with only one match of the league calendar remaining and just one place in the Champions League left up for grabs, Leverkusen welcomed Stuttgart to the BayArena safe in the knowledge that only one final victory would be enough to overhaul Stuttgart's two point lead on them going into the game. After a goalless first hour, Leverkusen won themselves a corner. As the ball was floated over, midfielder Carsten Ramelow found himself in space at the back post to head the ball back across the box to Franca who in turn nodded the ball goalwards towards Berbatov. The potent Bulgarian swivelled and acrobatically volleyed home the vital first goal to send Leverkusen's fans wild with delight.

Despite leading 1-0 through Berbatov's 16th goal of the season, Leverkusen were aware that an equaliser for Stuttgart would spell the end of the Rhineland club's dreams of Champions League football the next season, instead relegating them to Europe's lesser competition, the UEFA Cup. However, with just five minutes of the match remaining Daniel Bierofka received the ball on the left hand side and burst into the opposition's goal area only to be upended by Stuttgart's Portuguese defender Fernando Meira. Penalty! Goalkeeper Hans-Jorg Butt stepped forward to accept the responsibility of wrapping up a crucial victory. And he struck his penalty well enough, but when the ball rebounded off the post it looked like an opportunity to finish Stuttgart off had gone begging. However, luckily for Butt, the ball evaded the on-rushing Stuttgart defenders and fell to Schneider who confidently steered the ball home to complete a victory worth millions to the club.

Leverkusen leapfrogged Stuttgart, who had spent the majority of the season in the top three to finish the season in the lucrative third place and thus earn themselves a place in the qualifying rounds of the next season's Champions League. In just one year, Augenthaler had completely reversed Leverkusen's fortunes on the pitch, turning them from relegation candidates the previous season into Champions League qualifiers. Furthermore, he had given Berbatov his chance to shine in the first team on a regular basis and the young Bulgarian had repaid him handsomely with a barrage of goals. He forged a prolific partnership with Franca to fire the team into the Champions League again.

One downside for Augenthaler though, was the end of season announcement that key centre-back Lucio had opted to jump ship. As Ballack and Ze Roberto had done before him, Lucio was to join Bavarian rivals Bayern Munich for £8 million after four seasons at the BayArena. But with Berbatov and Franca beginning to find the net with increasing regularity and Champions

League football set to return to the BayArena, there were many reasons for the Leverkusen faithful to retain optimistic ahead of the 2004–05 campaign.

CHAPTER 6

THE MAIN MAN

'The game is about glory, doing things in style.'
SPURS LEGEND DANNY BLANCHFLOWER

Having scored a more than respectable 16 league goals to finish the previous campaign as Leverkusen's top scorer, Berbatov entered the 2004–05 campaign looking to build on the excellent partnership he had forged with the Brazilian Franca in both the Bundesliga and the Champions League.

During the summer there had been rumours of interest in obtaining the Bulgarian's services from several top clubs. And Leverkusen assistant secretary Ilya Kaentzik admitted in the *Daily Mail* in May 2004 that Celtic – where his international colleague Stilian Petrov was starring – had been monitoring Berbatov's progress with Leverkusen closely over the course of the 2003–04 season. However, Kaentzik also warned any potential suitors, including Celtic, that they wouldn't get the supremely gifted striker on the cheap after the club tied him to a new long-term contract to remain at the BayArena:

'There are already some big clubs interested. I know Celtic are looking at him, but we want to wait until after Euro 2004 to see if he explodes on to the competition the way he has done in the Bundesliga. Barcelona and Inter Milan are also hot on Dimitar, but they say it is too early for them to sign him. That gives Celtic a chance, but we have just secured Berbatov on a new four-year extended contract. He is a special talent and will not go cheaply.'

And although Bulgaria flopped badly at the European Championships in Portugal during the summer, losing all three games that they participated in, Berbatov was one of the few players from the team to come away from the tournament with his reputation still intact. And to the relief of the Leverkusen fans none of the team rumoured to have been interested in signing the Bulgarian backed up their interest in him with a firm bid, which meant the striker's short-term future at least remained at the BayArena. After managing to hold on to his number one forward, Klaus Augenthaler set about the task of freshening up the existing squad at his disposal by bringing in exciting German international winger Paul Freier from Bochum, Brazilian defender Roque Junior from Milan to replace the already departed Lucio, and Ukrainian forward Andriy Voronin from Leverkusen's relegated arch-rivals Cologne to supplement his attacking options.

Somewhat surprisingly though, of the players permitted to depart the club by Augenthaler, the biggest casualty was experienced German international striker

Olivier Neuville, who despite spending the majority of the previous season playing second fiddle to Berbatov and Franca, had still chipped in with some valuable goals for the team. Neuville departed for Borussia Monchengladbach while the talented Turkish schemer Yildiray Basturk headed for the German capital to join Hertha Berlin.

Leverkusen kicked off the new season at the BayArena with a 2-1 victory over Hannover. Although they went behind after conceding a goal with just 14 minutes of the match gone, the team bounced back after half-time to take all three points with goals from Bernd Schneider and a last gasp winner from Franca. And they followed up their opening day victory with a convincing 5-0 demolition of Czech side, Banik Ostrava, in their Champions League first leg qualifying tie courtesy of a hat-trick from Franca. Berbatov also got on the scoresheet to open his account for the season in the comprehensive victory.

The following weekend, Berbatov opened his league account for the season when he put Leverkusen back on level terms after the team went a goal behind at Bochum. Bochum regained the lead soon after, but with just three minutes of the match remaining, new signing Voronin announced himself to the travelling support with an important equaliser. Next up was the vitally important midweek Champions League second leg qualifier with Banik Ostrava in the Czech Republic, and the following weekend's clash with Felix Magath's star-studded Bayern Munich squad.

A third goal of the season from Berbatov wasn't

enough to prevent the team going down to a 2-1 defeat in Ostrava, but Leverkusen progressed to the lucrative group stages easily nevertheless by virtue of their emphatic 5-0 first leg victory. And in the resultant draw Leverkusen were assigned the difficult task of facing 2002 conquerors Real Madrid, Ukrainian giants Dynamo Kyiv and Italian outfit AS Roma, for a place in the knock out stages.

It turned out to be a terrible first return to the BayArena for Lucio the next weekend, however, as Augenthaler's rampant Leverkusen side ran out easy 4-1 winners over Bayern Munich on the day. Franca supplied Berbatov with the first when his probing pass carved open the Bayern defence to allow the Bulgarian to slide his shot past Oliver Kahn and into the net despite the last-ditch efforts of England international Owen Hargreaves. Leading 1-0 at half-time, Leverkusen doubled their lead soon after the second half restart when Berbatov and Franca combined to play a neat one-two which allowed the Brazilian the time to curl home a precise shot into the top corner of the net and out of Kahn's reach.

Franca grabbed his second goal of the match soon after when he outpaced fellow countryman, Lucio, to fire Leverkusen into a commanding 3-0 lead just before the hour. And, after some exquisite interplay between Robson Ponte, Franca and Berbatov, the Bulgarian found himself in acres of space to hammer a fourth past a bemused Kahn to complete a sensational seven minutes for the home side. Ballack headed home a fine late goal for Bayern, as he continued his run of scoring against his former club, but it proved scant consolation for the Bavarians as Leverkusen cemented their early-season title aspirations in style to go top of the early Bundesliga table going into September.

After disposing of title favourites Bayern Munich with consummate ease, Leverkusen were expected to go to freshly promoted western Rhineland neighbours Mainz and overpower them easily. However, Mainz clearly hadn't read the script and with Leverkusen perhaps guilty of having one eye on their forthcoming midweek Champions League clash with Real Madrid, Augenthaler's side fell to an embarrassing 2-0 defeat.

The defeat appeared to have little bearing on the team's preparations for the huge Champions League match with Madrid though, as they turned in an outstanding performance to romp to a 3-0 win with goals from Polish international midfielder Jacek Krzynowek – who fired a rocket past Iker Casillas in the Real goal – Franca and Berbatov sealing an impressive win and a large slice of revenge for the team's Champions League final defeat two years earlier.

Yet despite being able to topple one of the world's biggest teams in Real Madrid, when Augenthaler's team returned to league action the following weekend, they looked like a totally different side, as they trailed 2-0 at the hands of lowly Nurnberg and looked to be heading towards another embarrassing defeat. But, with the clock counting down towards the final whistle, Leverkusen redeemed themselves when they won a penalty which Hans-Jorg Butt calmly converted to halve the home side's lead. Then Berbatov ensured the

Rhineland club would return home with a point when he popped up with a last gasp equaliser to take his tally for the season to an impressive seven goals despite it still only being mid-September.

After the win over Madrid, Leverkusen travelled to the Ukraine to face domestic champions Dynamo Kyiv in their second match of the Champions League group stages, but despite holding a 2-1 advantage with just over 20 minutes left to play, Leverkusen collapsed under the pressure put on them by the hosts and conceded three goals to lose 4-2 on the night. And, new signing, Voronin, so keen to impress on his return to his homeland, summed up a frustrating night for the visitors as a whole when he lost his cool and was given his marching orders with only minutes of the match remaining.

And Leverkusen's inconsistent early season form continued when they were trounced 3-0 the following weekend at the hands of former German midfielder Matthias Sammer's Stuttgart side. However, the team managed to bounce back immediately in their very next Bundesliga match, when they took Hamburg apart to win 3-0 at the BayArena. Krzynowek got the ball rolling with a goal in the 10th minute before a goal from Brazilian defender Juan, and another from Berbatov sealed a welcome victory to leave the club in sixth position the Bundesliga at the start of October.

And the young Bulgarian's tremendous start to the season continued when he helped himself to three goals in two games while on international duty for his country. These were the early fixtures of the qualifying campaign for the 2006 World Cup to be held in Germany. After returning to Germany and club duty, though, the in-form striker was unable to do anything about Leverkusen's third defeat of the season, as the team slipped to a disappointing 3-1 loss at the hands of Hertha Berlin in the German capital. Yet the team's fortunes in Europe proved to be in complete contrast to their form in the Bundesliga when goals from Robson Ponte, Krzynowek and Franca secured Leverkusen an impressive home win over AS Roma in the Champions League, their second of the competition.

The victory in Europe appeared to boost the team's flagging confidence in the league, when they narrowly won a close-fought victory over Arminia Bielefeld 3-2 thanks to a superb hat-trick from new signing Voronin. The team travelled to nearby Dortmund looking to make it two wins from two the following weekend, but yet again the team's inconsistent early season form returned to haunt them as they lost by a single goal at the Westfalenstadion, to finish October languishing in mid-table.

Leverkusen then travelled to the 'eternal city' of Rome to face a Roma side also sitting rather miserably in mid-table obscurity following their own lacklustre start to the season. In addition, following an incident at the Stadio Olimpico in Roma's previous match against Dynamo Kyiv which left match referee Anders Frisk nursing a bloodied forehead after being struck by a missile thrown from the crowd, Roma were forced by UEFA to play their home match against Leverkusen behind closed doors.

The game appeared to be heading for a relatively unmemorable stalemate, until Berbatov received the ball on the edge of the area with just under 10 minutes of the contest remaining. Having been left isolated for the majority of the game up front as the lone striker, the Bulgarian suddenly burst into life when he received possession on the left hand side. On receiving the ball he flicked it up over his shoulder to leave Roma defender Dellas a helpless spectator before cushioning a lovely lob over the advancing goalkeeper to give Leverkusen a priceless lead in the eerily empty stadium. It was a sublime goal – one of his best ever – the type of goal kids dream about scoring in the school playground. Although Vincenzo Montella equalised in stoppage time for the *Giallorossi*, it proved too little too late for the team from the Italian capital as they crashed out of Europe at the group stage. Meanwhile, the point, won courtesy of Berbatov's wonder-goal, ensured Leverkusen retained a good chance of qualifying from the group as they sat level on points with Madrid and Dynamo Kyiv.

Back on the domestic front, Leverkusen returned to winning ways with a commanding 4-1 success over Freiburg at the BayArena, ahead of their clash with reigning Bundesliga champions, Werder Bremen in the north west of Germany. German international striker, Miroslav Klose got Bremen off to good start when he put the hosts ahead after 20 minutes, but Leverkusen showed fighting spirit to haul themselves back into the game and take the lead when Voronin and Berbatov scored within the space of two second-half minutes. An upset appeared to be on the cards but Bremen rallied to equalise with 20 minutes of the match remaining.

A disheartening 3-0 reverse followed when Leverkusen

were put to the sword by nearby rivals Schalke at the BayArena – not the ideal preparation ahead of a daunting trip to the Bernabeu to face Real Madrid in a crucial Champions League group game. However, frustratingly for their fans and Augenthaler, Leverkusen showed once again that they were able to step up a gear each time they faced a Champions League match, as they earned a fantastic 1-1 draw in the Spanish capital. However, it could have been so much better for the German side if they had only been able to hold onto the lead that had been given to them yet again by their ever-reliable goalscoring machine from Bulgaria. Instead though, Raul's equaliser 20 minutes from time meant the team would need to beat Dynamo Kyiv at the BayArena to emerge from the group and into the knock out stages of the competition.

A 2-0 victory over Hansa Rostock followed courtesy of goals from Berbatov – his sixth league goal of the season – and Voronin. But with the mid-season break just around the corner, the team stumbled into December lying in a disappointing 10th place in the league, yet strangely only five points off the third position which guaranteed the incumbent the chance of Champions League football the following season. However, if Augenthaler's men retained any thoughts of making that third place their own, they would have to start producing results quickly on the pitch. And they began December as they finished November with a victory, as the team came from one goal down within four minutes of kick-off against Wolfsburg, to secure a 2-1 victory thanks to Franca's last minute winning goal.

Leverkusen ensured they would make it into the draw for the knock out stages of the Champions League as group winners when they scored three second half goals to ward off Kyiv's challenge at the BayArena. However, at one stage it appeared that Leverkusen would most likely go into their second round match minus their star striker from Bulgaria. After a great start to the 2004–05 campaign, Berbatov was reportedly attracting interest from Liverpool's new manager Rafa Benitez, who was on the look out for a top class striker to lead the line at Anfield following the departure of fans' favourite Michael Owen to Real Madrid the previous summer. Berbatov reportedly fitted the bill perfectly. And Leverkusen indicated that they were willing to sell the popular forward to the Merseyside giants, but when the two clubs were drawn to play each other in the Champions League second round, Leverkusen backed out of the deal and Liverpool signed Fernando Morientes from Real Madrid instead.

Three days after the Kyiv win, Leverkusen looked to be heading into the winter break with another victory under their belts against lowly Borussia Monchengladbach. Berbatov again took the responsibility of scoring the majority of Leverkusen's goals on his young but broad shoulders, only for the team to be pegged back by a penalty award which was successfully converted. With 17 matches played, Leverkusen's lay in eighth position in the league at the mid-season break, yet only eight points behind league leaders Bayern Munich and Schalke. And with a second round Champions League tie against Benitez's Liverpool to look forward to, and Berbatov confidently banging in the goals left, right and centre, there was much optimism among the fans that the club could achieve something special that season.

January 2005 proved to be an immensely embarrassing and shameful time for German football. Leverkusen had begun the second half of the campaign with a brilliant 3-0 away victory over Hannover, the goals coming from Voronin, Freier and Berbatov, who began the new year as he had finished the old. However, the weekend's Bundesliga fixtures were hugely overshadowed by major revelations of a match-fixing scandal operating in Germany involving match referees and an illegal Croatian betting mafia. With Germany now in the vital preparation stages for the 2006 World Cup, the timing of the revelations could hardly have been worse.

Away from the politics of the game and back on the football field, Leverkusen followed up their 3-0 win over Hannover with a fabulous 4-0 thumping of Bochum as Augenthaler's men set about the task of climbing the table. But their scintillating new year form came crashing back down the following weekend when the team travelled to Munich to face Bayern. A 2-0 defeat stretched Bayern's lead over them to nine points. It meant it would take a massive effort for Augenthaler's young team to claw back such a hefty points difference to challenge for the Bundesliga title.

Next up, the team exacted sweet revenge over Mainz for their early season defeat with a 2-0 victory, and a 4-2 away win over Nurnberg the next weekend ensured Leverkusen's confidence levels remained high ahead of the vital Champions League first leg at Anfield. Berbatov in particular delivered the impression that he could pose the biggest threat to the Merseyside giants in midweek, when he helped himself to a brace of goals as Leverkusen swept Nurnberg aside after being pegged back to 2-2 at one stage of the game.

Ahead of the Champions League tie at Anfield, Berbatov spoke in *The Times* about his hopes of progressing to the quarter-finals: 'I remember playing against Liverpool. We beat them but it was a terrific game, so exciting, and at one stage they were ahead on away goals. But we came through it only to lose in the final. It was a great experience and I think we are better equipped this time around. Everything at the club is perfectly set up for success and that is our aim. We want to repeat our victory against Liverpool. We are stronger mentally than we were. We are less likely to lose games late on than before and we are confident that we can beat anyone on our day, as was proved when we beat Real Madrid 3-0 (in the first match of the group stage in September). We have watched a lot of their games this season and as well as being their captain, Gerrard is the team's real leader. But they have other good players and Rafa Benitez is a good coach, so we know the games will be tough. It's hard to predict whether history can repeat itself, but if we do well in the first leg, I think we have a chance of progressing at home.'

However, despite going into the match high in confidence and determined that they could repeat their feat of two seasons earlier, Leverkusen came unstuck at Anfield when Luis Garcia opened the scoring for the *Reds*. Then free-kicks from John Arne Riise and German international midfielder Didi Hamann looked to have sewn up the tie for the four-time European champions ahead of the second leg at the BayArena. Despite playing on the backfoot for the majority of the game and with time running out for Leverkusen to salvage anything from the match, the team made one last foray into the Liverpool half to grab what appeared to be a vital away goal through Franca.

Back in the league, Leverkusen appeared to have stolen a late win against Stuttgart at the BayArena when Berbatov found the target again to open the scoring after 80 minutes. But Stuttgart hit back with a late goal of their own when the Brazilian striker Cacau fired home in the last minute. That goal prevented Leverkusen from moving up to fourth in the table. And the team failed to gain the morale-boosting win they so desperately required the week after, too, when they lost 1-0 to Hamburg.

And so, two weeks after their first leg win, Liverpool travelled to the BayArena in midweek looking to finish the job they had started at Anfield. Leverkusen meanwhile needed to go all out for a win in order to try and peg back the two-goal lead held by their more illustrious visitors from the north west of England. However, two goals in four first half minutes from pint-sized Liverpool forward Luis Garcia ensured Liverpool would be in the draw for the quarter-finals at Leverkusen's expense. After just 32 minutes of play, Berbatov's day went from bad to worse when he was forced to leave the pitch early after sustaining an injury against the team that had come so close to signing him before Christmas. Milan Baros added a third to compound Leverkusen's misery midway through the second half, before Leverkusen bowed out of the competition with a consolation goal of their own through Krzynowek.

With Leverkusen's participation in Europe over for another season, Augenthaler's team sought to get back to winning ways in the league when they welcomed Hertha Berlin to the BayArena. But with only six minutes of the match remaining, Leverkusen found themselves trailing 3-2, only for Voronin to pop up with a crucial equaliser to keep Leverkusen's hopes of a place in European competition the following season alive. With the season beginning to approach its climax, Leverkusen welcomed Kaiserslautern to the BayArena knowing that a victory over them was absolutely vital to keep them in the hunt for a top five finish. And a 2-0 win ensured they didn't lose any further ground on Bremen and Hertha Berlin who were currently occupying fourth and fifth spots in the league.

But just as it seemed that Leverkusen were ready to put in a strong challenge to the sides directly above them in the table, the team crashed to a frustrating defeat at the hands of Arminia Bielefeld. And a 1-0 defeat at Dortmund further dented Leverkusen's hopes of European football the next season, although they did bounce back to beat already relegated Freiburg 3-1 with Berbatov getting his name on the scoresheet twice. And they followed up the victory with another important win, this time over fellow European challengers Werder Bremen, 2-1.

With only four matches of the Bundesliga season remaining, Berbatov and his colleagues made the short journey to Gelsenkirschen to face championship challengers Schalke as they looked to put a dent in the title aspirations of their close neighbours in order to keep themselves in touch with the teams directly above them in the standings. However, things looked bleak at half time as they trailed 3-1. But not for the first time in the season, Berbatov came to Leverkusen's rescue when he pulled a goal back ten minutes after half time. And only minutes after Berbatov had reduced the arrears, Voronin netted to bring the two teams level, leaving Leverkusen lying in sixth position in the table just three points behind Werder Bremen and Hertha Berlin and just five points behind third placed Stuttgart.

With just three games left to play, Leverkusen went into the match with Hansa Rostock at the BayArena aware knowing that any result other than victory could mean a season without European football for only the second time since the mid-1990s. However, any concerns the fans may have had were quickly dispelled by the ever-reliable Berbatov who put the home team a goal ahead with just over 25 minutes of the match played. Voronin, with whom Berbatov had struck up a fruitful partnership since his arrival in the summer, added a second after half-time and the Bulgarian added a third two minutes from time as Leverkusen ensured Rostock's relegation from the top flight of German football. With Bayern Munich confirmed as champions for the 19th time, Leverkusen were still aiming to secure European qualification with two games of the season remaining. Bremen's defeat away at Borussia Dortmund meant there was only goal difference separating the two teams now.

A 2-2 draw for Leverkusen away at Wolfsburg and a 4-1 victory over Freiburg for Werder Bremen, allowed Bremen to move two points clear in the race for the Champions League qualifiers. And despite a 5-1 victory for Leverkusen over Borussia Monchengladbach – including a magnificent 20-minute hat-trick from Berbatov to take his goal tally to 20 goals for the season from 32 matches – Werder Bremen won away at Kaiserslautern to secure Champions League football for the 2005–06 season ahead of Hertha Berlin and Stuttgart.

The 2004/05 campaign was certainly one to remember for Dimitar Berbatov. For the second season in succession he had finished the season as Leverkusen's top goalscorer firing them into the qualifying rounds of the UEFA Cup and for the first time in his professional career he had reached the magical 20-goal mark for a single campaign. He also enjoyed a fine run in the Champions League as he scored five goals in 10 games to help Leverkusen topple some of Europe's biggest teams. The question that was on everyone's lips though was – would he stay or would he go? After all, there had been interest aplenty during the mid-season break. After seeing Bayern Munich cherry-pick the cream of their players in recent seasons, Leverkusen's fans prayed that Berbatov would remain at the BayArena for at least one more season, and spurn any overtures received. But the decision would ultimately rest with the club and Berbatov himself.

After a summer off to consider his options, Berbatov decided to remain at the BayArena for at least one more season, at which point he would look at the situation again. Meanwhile, Augenthaler decided to strengthen his squad for the season ahead by signing talented youngsters Simon Rolfes from Aachen, Tranquillo Barnetta from Hannover and the Brazilian Athirson from Cruzeiro while there were also a number of high-profile departures including the transfer of Daniel Bierofka to Stuttgart, Franca to J-League club Kashiwa Reysol, Robson Ponte to Urawa Red Diamonds also of the J-League in Japan and Diego Placente who departed for Celta Vigo in Spain.

Leverkusen ran out on the first day of the new season to face Eintracht Frankfurt with a steely determination to get their campaign off to a good start. Yet, they did anything but early on as Frankfurt took an early lead with just seven minutes of the new season played. However, less than 20 minutes later, it was Berbatov who opened the Leverkusen scoring for the season, to drag his team level. And further goals in the second half from Voronin, Bernd Schneider and Krzynowek, ensured Leverkusen finished the match with maximum points from their first game of the new campaign.

Next up for Leverkusen was a visit from champions Bayern Munich to the BayArena. Last season they had given Bayern an early season battering by 4-1. But this time things proved to be different and the match got off to the worst possible start for the home team when former Leverkusen midfielder Michael Ballack shot Bayern into the lead with only minutes on the clock. Then Roy Makaay doubled the lead with just 11 minutes played. Berbatov pulled a goal back after half an hour as he tucked away a cool penalty following a foul from

Oliver Kahn. But the day belonged to Bayern and Makaay in particular as the Dutch striker completed a hat trick in the second half to inspire the champions to a devastating 5-2 away victory.

A defeat in the club's next game away at Wolfsburg coupled with a 1-1 draw at home to Schalke and a first round UEFA Cup defeat at the hands of Berbatov's former club in Bulgaria, CSKA Sofia, resulted in the parting of ways between Leverkusen and their coach Klaus Augenthaler in mid-September after two years in the job. Augenthaler hadn't done himself any favours with the club's hierarchy in the summer when he criticized the policy of moving players on without buying suitable replacements. He had earned himself a warning for his comment: 'You don't sell a Ponte, Placente, Bierofka and Franca and then talk about reaching the Champions League.' With the downturn in results and the team's apparent lack of confidence, the board voted unanimously to remove Augenthaler from his position as head coach at the club. Rudi Voller, the club's sports director and former head ocach of the national team commented: 'We felt we couldn't go on in this vein. We were not playing with any purpose. The belief had disappeared.'

Voller took over temporary control of the club in the aftermath of the sacking before the job of head coach was bestowed upon Voller's right-hand man during his time as Germany coach, Michael Skibbe. Following the departure of Augenthaler, Leverkusen's fortunes appeared to alter as Berbatov notched a fifth goal in his fifth match of the season to help his team-mates to a comfortable 3-1 win over newly-promoted Duisburg. But the team lost again to CSKA Sofia to see them eliminated in the first round of the UEFA Cup. A win over Cologne, promoted back to the Bundesliga a season after going down, followed before defeats in late September and early October left Leverkusen sitting in mid-table obscurity, and already 11 points behind the pacesetters at the top of the table, Bayern Munch and Werder Bremen.

The remainder of October didn't get much better for the club either as Leverkusen continued to freefall down the table as they fell way off the pace set by Bayern Munich. Even Berbatov's goals were in short supply now and, following two draws in a row before a late own goal gifted the team a 2-1 victory over Dortmund at the BayArena, it looked more likely that Leverkusen would be fighting to avoid the drop come the end of the season rather than fighting to win a place in Europe. A disappointing draw away at Monchengladbach followed before dismal defeats at the hands of Hamburg and Hertha Berlin despite a goal from Berbatov.

In the meantime, Berbatov once again became the subject of transfer speculation in 2005 when it was revealed that he had a 15 million euro get-out clause written into his contract. And despite the fact that the club were hoping to keep hold of their star player, Leverkusen general manager Michael Reschke told the newspaper *Kolner Express*: 'We want to build a great team with Berbatov but it is not entirely in our hands. It is true that there is a get-out clause in his contract. We do not want to let him go but we know that if the likes of AC Milan or Real Madrid come knocking we cannot compete and just have to look for a replacement.'

Back on the pitch, Leverkusen went into the mid-season break on the back of two further lacklustre draws against Nurnberg and Hannover to leave them lying in 12th place at the mid-season point and a massive 25 points behind league leaders Bayern Munich.

Two days before Christmas Berbatov picked up the accolade of Bulgarian Player of the Year for the second year in a row and third time overall after a fantastic season which saw him finish in the Bundesliga's top three goalscorers. Speaking at the awards ceremony back in Bulgaria, Berbatov said: 'This means a lot to me'.

When the Bundesliga resumed in late January, Leverkusen scraped a 2-1 victory over Frankfurt in their first game after the winter break, before succumbing to a 1-0 defeat at the hands of Bayern Munich that ensured the Bavarian club did the double over Leverkusen.

February proved to be a good month for Berbatov as he found his shooting boots once again to fire four goals home for Leverkusen, as the Rhineland club won three of its five matches, with the only loss being a remarkable 7-4 defeat in Gelsenkirchen at the hands of Schalke. However, despite the team's upsurge in form, they were still lying 26 points behind leaders Bayern Munich and 18 behind second and third placed teams Werder Bremen and Hamburg. It didn't take a genius to realise that Berbatov would look at making a move away from Leverkusen in the summer transfer window. Leverkusen couldn't compete with the big teams around Europe when it came to fanbase, ground size, transfer budget and wage rises. Berbatov needed to be playing at a bigger and better club.

In last two months of the 2005/06 season, Berbatov scored a barrage of goals to finish his fifth full season in the Rhineland with 21 goals in 34 appearances guiding Leverkusen to a sixth place finish in the Bundesliga and another season in the UEFA Cup. The only question that remained to be answered now, was where would he end up playing next season?

CHAPTER 7
LONDON CALLING

'Any player coming to Spurs, whether he's a big signing or just a ground staff boy, must be dedicated to the game and to the club. He must never be satisfied with his last performance and he must hate losing ... Spurs have got to be the best in the land, not the second best.'

FORMER SPURS MANAGER BILL NICHOLSON

Legend has it in certain areas of North London that when the final digit of the year ends in a one, it will be a trophy-laden year for Tottenham Hotspur Football Club. For example, the 1950-51 season saw Spurs finish as Football League champions while the 1960-61 campaign saw them achieve an even greater feat as the club completed a glorious season as double winners under the guidance of Scottish manager, Bill Nicholson.

They also won the FA Cup in 1901, 1921 and 1991 but perhaps most famously in 1981, when inspired by 'that' glorious solo goal from Argentine import Ricky Villa, Spurs defeated Manchester City 3-2 in only the second cup final to go to a replay at Wembley. Earlier that same year, far away from North London in a small city in the south-west of Bulgaria, a child was born who some 26 years later would become the object of the

White Hart Lane faithful's affections. His name? Dimitar Ivanov Berbatov.

With another season as Leverkusen's top scorer complete and the team safely qualified for the UEFA Cup from a fifth place finish in the Bundesliga, the loyal fans of the club from the Rhineland were bracing themselves for the inevitable departure of their number one striker to pastures new. After plying his trade in the Germany for the previous five-and-a-half seasons, Berbatov's time at Leverkusen was drawing to a close. He was in need of a new challenge, a new style of football, a new way of life.

For the past three campaigns he had finished as Leverkusen's top goalscorer and also as one of the top goalscorers in the Bundesliga. And, his stock had risen so rapidly in his last three seasons at the club that when it became common knowledge that Leverkusen were prepared to listen to offers for their star player, Berbatov's signature was rumoured to have been coveted by a number of Europe's biggest clubs.

To the shock of many experts however, Leverkusen sprang something of a surprise when the club's sporting director, Rudi Voller, publicly announced that a deal was close to completion with Tottenham Hotspur Football Club for the Bulgarian's transfer. None of the world's leading media outlets had predicted such an unexpected turn of events. It had been the popular belief that Berbatov would be gracing one of Serie A or La Liga's biggest amphitheatres at the start of the 2005/06 season, or at least one of the Premier League's 'big four'. But Spurs? Surely it had to be a mistake.

Yet, despite the consternation expressed towards this

most unlikely of destinations, there was no mistake. Voller admitted to the German newspaper *Bild* on 11 May 2006 that a deal had been struck for the Bulgarian's transfer. He said: 'Tottenham have been in contact and are now prepared to pay the transfer fee we are asking for. It is now Dimitar's decision. It is understandable that he wants to see something different after six years in Leverkusen. But it hurts us to lose a class player.'

And Leverkusen head coach, Michael Skibbe, confirmed the Bay Arena fans' worst fears when he admitted dejectedly that a deal was almost complete: 'It looks as if Berbo could leave us.'

And so, the summer of 2006 began encouragingly for supporters of sleeping giant Tottenham Hotspur, when with the previous season barely over the club announced the exciting signing of Berbatov for a hefty fee of £10.9 million, the first Bulgarian footballer to ever sign for Spurs. But who was he? Where was he from? Was he any good? £10.9 million was a lot of money for a relatively unknown player. Would he be worth it? Would he score the goals that would take Spurs into the Promised Land – the highly-lucrative Champions League? All sorts of questions were being asked by the White Hart Lane faithful upon hearing the news that Tottenham head coach Martin Jol had just splashed out nearly £11 million of his close season budget on the relatively unknown Bulgarian international forward.

The German Bundesliga is something of unknown quantity to English football fans. It doesn't receive a great deal of media coverage, written or televised, unlike its Italian and Spanish counterparts, who in recent years have seen their matches televised increasingly by broadcasters in the UK. Hence, German football is widely perceived by Britons as defensive and uneasy on the eye.

A number of the White Hart Lane regulars were sceptical about the move, or rather the fee. And perhaps it was with some justification that they felt concern. After all, for many, Sergiy Rebrov's ill-fated stay in North London still remained fresh in the memory. In June 2000, George Graham, the then manager of Spurs, had parted company with £11 million pounds to secure the club record signing of eastern European superstar Rebrov from Dynamo Kiev. The transfer represented something of a coup for Spurs, the prolific marksman having formed half of one of the most feared striking partnerships in Europe alongside Andriy Shevchenko at both Kiev and the Ukraine throughout the 1990s. Rebrov's signature, like Berbatov's, had been coveted by a number of Europe's biggest clubs, while a reunification with Shevchenko – who had left Kiev at the end of the previous season to join Italian giants AC Milan – had also been mooted.

However, Graham managed to persuade Rebrov that he could be a vital piece of the jigsaw and help Spurs challenge the 'big four's' dominance for regular silverware once again. Upon hearing Graham's plans, the Ukrainian duly signed on the dotted line for the North London club. But while Shevchenko prospered in the cosmopolitan city of Milan, finishing his first season in Serie A as overall top goalscorer, Rebrov wasn't so fortunate at Spurs, then under the stewardship of Spurs legend Glenn Hoddle after Graham's departure in 2001. He left Spurs in 2005 after two seasons out on loan at Fenerbahce and West Ham, having made just 76 appearances for the Tottenham first team, scoring 16 goals in the process.

Berbatov's goal-scoring record at the Rhineland-based club in the west of Germany certainly looked impressive. And despite their scepticism, Spurs' fans crossed their fingers he would be able to replicate his touch and fire them to overdue success. He already held a distinct advantage over the Ukrainian in that he spoke fluent English upon his arrival in North London. Berbatov was a huge fan of gangster movies and in particular the *Godfather* trilogy starring Robert de Niro. And he also has all James Bond films which enabled him to learn English to a level which would make transition to life in the UK easier.

With the purchase of Berbatov, Spurs possessed four top-class strikers with Robbie Keane, Jermain Defoe and the Egyptian Mido, who made his loan deal from Italian giants AS Roma permanent. Jol had identified 25-year-old Berbatov as the man to take the club to the next level and give the fans what they desired most: Champions League football and trophies to add to their glorious triumphs.

Yet four strikers would be vying for two starting berths in all probability. Would Jol be able to rotate the quartet enough to keep them all happy? Having four top forwards was a tactic that had served Sir Alex Ferguson so well in 1999, when his own forward quartet of Andy Cole, Dwight Yorke, Ole Gunnar Solskjaer and former

Spur Teddy Sheringham, had fired Manchester United to their glorious treble. Would the tactic work for Jol? Would he be able to keep all four happy? Only time would tell.

Speaking for the first time to the club's official website, Berbatov spoke of his delight at completing a dream move to the English Premier League: 'Tottenham is a club that is building something special. The squad has some terrific young players, an excellent manager and coaching staff and I am looking forward to playing my part.'

With the signing complete, Spurs' sporting director Damien Comolli spoke of the club's joy at securing the talented striker on a four-year contract, revealing that Spurs had beaten off tough competition to land the prolific striker: 'There were a number of clubs interested in signing Dimitar, clubs from France, Spain and the Premiership. We are delighted he has chosen to join us.'

Meanwhile Berbatov revealed to BBC Sport that Spurs had been trailing him for quite some time before the transfer was finally completed. He said: 'I've watched Spurs for a couple of months, how they play and have grown, and I hope to do something special here. They tried to buy me in January but Leverkusen said no. Spurs waited and have now signed me. I came here to try to do my best with guys in the team.'

The fans may not have known much about him upon his arrival, but one Spurs player who had come up against Berbatov on numerous occasions during his own time playing in the German Bundesliga with Werder Bremen, Paul Stalteri, admitted his delight upon hearing of head coach Martin Jol's latest signing. In an interview with the official club website, the Canadian defender enthused: 'I always thought Dimitar was one of the best strikers in the Bundesliga. He scores goals and was a handful every time I played against Bayer Leverkusen. He was certainly one of the best I came up against during my time in Germany.'

However, things could have turned out so differently for the Bulgarian. In an exclusive interview with *World Soccer*, Berbatov admitted that he had turned down the chance to join north-west giants Manchester United in favour of a move to Spurs, following a conversation with Spurs boss Martin Jol. Such a statement was sure to get the instant approval of the club's loyal support. He also admitted his desire to help Spurs qualify for the Champions League for the first time after the club had missed out on the feat at the final hurdle the previous season, when an illness-stricken side lost agonizingly to West Ham.

Berbatov said: 'I can reveal now that I had an offer from Manchester United and everyone knows what it means but after talking to Martin several times I decided to choose Spurs.'

Berbatov wouldn't be the only new face to join in with pre-season training at the start of July however, as Spurs completed the signings of left-back Benoit Assou-Ekotto from French club RC Lens and Didier Zokora from St Etienne after an impressive showing for the Ivory Coast during the summer's World Cup in Germany.

After spending a few days training and getting to know the rest of the squad who had not been representing their countries at the World Cup, Berbatov spoke to the official website about his happiness at being back on the training field after a summer off: 'I am finding it good, it is training again, but I like that. It is hard, but I prefer it like that.'

And the Bulgarian lined up for his new club for the first time when the club travelled to the south of France for a short pre-season tour beginning with a match against Girondins Bordeaux. Partnering Jermain Defoe up front, Berbatov made a low-key debut as Spurs kicked off the tour with a 2-1 victory, but he did give an indication of things to come when he flashed a second half shot just wide of the post before departing with ten minutes of the match remaining. The Bulgarian sat out the next game, a 1-0 victory over Nice, but returned to play 45 second half minutes in the 2-0 victory over Spanish outfit Celta Vigo.

With the World Cup attendees now back in training, Spurs travelled to the Midlands and St. Andrews to face Birmingham City in their first pre-season match on English soil. And it proved to be a special day for Berbatov as he grabbed two goals to signal his arrival in English football and to the travelling hordes of Spurs fans. He opened the scoring on 12 minutes after receiving a pass from Robbie Keane – something the Spurs fans would become used to over time – before turning in a flash to fire home his first goal for his new club.

Two minutes later he doubled the lead in stunning fashion when he latched onto a long ball forward before hammering an unstoppable shot past Maik Taylor between the Birmingham posts. The Bulgarian nearly completed a superb hat-trick in the second half but saw an effort flash just wide of the goal. But in the space of just 70 minutes he had already given an indication of what a valuable player he would prove to be in the season ahead.

After a wonderful debut on English soil, Berbatov revealed his delight at getting off the mark so early in his Spurs career: 'Not a bad start at all! For me personally it was great to score two goals and for my team to win, I thought we played well and deserved to win. It is important. You don't want to go two or three games without scoring but, when an opportunity comes, everything is okay again. Luckily for me I have scored now and I hope to continue in the same way.'

The new man notched his third goal of an impressive pre-season as Spurs comfortably defeated Stevenage Borough 3-0 in their next warm up match. But only days later and to the utter dismay of the fans, Spurs made the announcement that England international Michael Carrick, a vital cog in the Spurs midfield for the past two seasons since joining from West Ham, had expressed his desire to leave and join Sir Alex Ferguson's Manchester United team.

Disappointed at his star midfielder's decision to abandon his emerging team, Jol said: 'This is a move that Michael wants to make. We have given him every reason to stay, but he has asked to be allowed to leave.' Despite his obvious disappointment at the loss of Carrick, Jol took time out of the club's busy pre-season schedule to assess how his new acquisitions had settled in at Spurs Lodge: 'They have to cope themselves with English football – I can help them – and with what we've seen so far, they are on the way. Benoit and Dimitar have done well in the friendlies and Dimitar has scored a couple of terrific goals. We lined-up Didier Zokora early and Benoit is a very good option as a left full-back but he could also play if necessary wide on the left.

'Dimitar was at the top of scoring charts in the Bundesliga with Miroslav Klose last season, he's a very good mover, a target man, a goal-scorer and we're very happy to have them all on board. If you look on the left we only had Young-Pyo Lee last season and now we have two options, in midfield we already had a few players but Carrick has gone and now Didier is here, we also have Edgar Davids, JJ, Tom Huddlestone and Teemu Tainio and up front Dimitar is here to give us his extra quality with his size, his touch and his overall play in the box. We are pretty satisfied.'

Spurs continued their fine pre-season form with a 2-1 victory over Inter Milan at the Lane and following the match club captain Ledley King gave his own verdict to the website on Jol's new signings: 'It is always difficult to tell how things are shaping up in pre-season because mostly you want to get fit and give the new players time to settle in and find their feet. We've been happy with what we've seen from them, we've made them feel welcome and I feel our squad is stronger for this season. Everyone is just looking forward to the season starting now.'

And speaking specifically about Berbatov's impact since arriving in the country, King, who had been ruled out of the rest of the pre-season campaign due to a knee injury, enthused: 'Obviously we have had a few weeks to work with him now and you can see what he is about in training. Although he didn't score in France, you knew it was just going to be a matter of time with him and it didn't take too long for him to make his mark at Birmingham with two great finishes. I am looking forward to playing with him in the league. He looks like a great finisher and I'm sure he is going to prove a great signing for the club.'

Berbatov showed off his excellent striking prowess once again on his first return to Germany since leaving Leverkusen, when he struck an excellent equaliser against Borussia Dortmund at the Westfalenstadion to keep Spurs' unbeaten pre-season intact. And the team finished their preparations for the new campaign with a 2-1 victory over Basque outfit Real Sociedad at the Lane a week ahead of their Premier League curtain-raiser at the Reebok Stadium against Bolton Wanderers.

As for Berbatov, four goals in his first pre-season at the club suggested those fans who had been openly sceptical about Jol's judgement had little to be concerned about. But scoring in pre-season friendlies and scoring in the Premier League are two different matters. However, they wouldn't have too long to wait to find out whether he was up to the challenge or not.

CHAPTER 8

SEASON TO REMEMBER

'Berba is a wonderful player, one of the best I've ever played alongside. His hold-up play is tremendous and for a big man, his touch is excellent, one of the best I've seen. He's also a great finisher as he's shown this season and a pleasure to play with.'
TOTTENHAM HOTSPUR FORWARD ROBBIE KEANE

After completing a highly successful pre-season schedule, Spurs travelled north to face Bolton at the Reebok Stadium in their first Premier League match of the season. Berbatov was named in the starting lineup to make his debut up front alongside Jermain Defoe, while fellow new recruits, Zokora and Assou-Ekotto were also picked to make debuts.

Before the match, Berbatov spoke to the club's official website of his excitement ahead of his debut: 'I'm excited – it feels like I've been waiting a long time for this game. It's my first Premiership game, my debut and maybe I'll have a few nerves as well but when I step onto the pitch all that will be forgotten and I will try to score goals for my team. It would be wonderful to score in the first game. It is the dream of every striker to score on his debut at a new club and after that to score and score again. I've been told that Bolton are a good team, I know a lot of their players by name and they play a physical style but we cannot be afraid. I respect their team but we go there looking to win.'

And his strike partner for the match, Defoe, revealed in the official match day programme his own excitement at the prospect of partnering the Bulgarian and his high hopes for a productive season: 'I knew from the first time I saw him in training, his movement and finishing are excellent and he is so clever. He holds up the ball well and is a target man. Not only that, he can play on the shoulder as well. He has done very well so far in the games he has played. He looks like a great signing.'

However, the trip proved a disappointing one for Berbatov and his new team-mates as the Lancashire club secured all three points thanks to an early goal from the head of the unmarked Kevin Davies and a 40-yard wonder strike from the Spanish veteran Ivan Campo. The Bulgarian hotshot struggled to impose himself on the game during his first competitive outing for the club and aside from one second half chance, where Bolton keeper Jussi Jaaskelainen was alert enough to thwart him, he was kept relatively quiet by Bolton's defence throughout. The 2-0 defeat extended Spurs' sorry record at the Reebok, which rose to no wins since the conception of the Premier League.

Despite the defeat, Jol reflected on the game as one that would have proved beneficial to Tottenham's new boys: 'It would have been a great experience for Benoit, Berbatov and especially Zokora in that midfield. It was "welcome to the Premiership" and they will benefit from that.'

After the match Berbatov, like his new boss, looked to take the positives out of his first match, albeit a defeat: 'They are a strong physical team. We have seen the first goal in the changing room though and it is clear there was a foul against us. We didn't play well and we will need to play better in the next game. We knew how they would play, we tried to counter it but unfortunately it didn't happen for us. They fought the whole time and we were not strong enough on the day, but our second game will be better.'

He also reflected on a missed opportunity to open his account for the club in competitive action: 'It was a good chance but the goalkeeper was very smart. We are all looking forward to Tuesday now, we want to win and make it up to the fans.'

The team had just three days to mull over their opening day defeat before getting the chance to win their first points of the season as they entertained newly promoted Sheffield United at the Lane. And it took Berbatov just seven minutes to signal his arrival to the home supporters when he accepted the simplest of tasks to tap home for his first competitive Spurs goal, following Aaron Lennon's teasing run and low cross from the right. Less than 10 minutes later Spurs doubled their advantage as Berbatov displayed another attribute of his game. A superb cushioned header from Robbie Keane's floated pass, fell into the path of the on-rushing Jermaine Jenas. JJ neatly chipped the advancing Paddy Kenny to give Spurs a comfortable 2-0 win.

Jol was understandably delighted as the team secured their first points of the season with relative ease: 'Robbie

Keane knew exactly how to play with Berbatov with their three at the back, and it was very pleasing for us that the lads did what we wanted and gave the crowd a performance. The final score doesn't reflect the game because we could have had three or four. That is the only thing we have to work on, to score more goals.'

And Keane, deputising as captain in the absence of the injured Ledley King, enthused about Berbatov's early strike: 'It will do his confidence the world of good. It is important as a striker to get off the mark and full credit to him – hopefully now he can continue it. He's been banging them in pre-season and in training. It was nice for him to get one in the league – especially in front our fans at home.'

Keane also reserved special praise for young wing wizard Lennon, who played a vital contribution to Berbatov's opening goal: 'Aaron has been on fire for a while now and he did exactly what we wanted from him again. He got wide, got at players, managed an assist and was brilliant.'

With their first three points on the board, Spurs played host to Everton the following weekend and almost took a first half lead as Gary Naysmith just about managed to clear Berbatov's goal-bound flick as the ball appeared destined to find the back of net. But despite enjoying the advantage of an extra man for two thirds of the match following Kevin Kilbane's sending off for two cautions, an unfortunate own goal from Calum Davenport and an Andy Johnson strike saw the Merseysiders return north with the points, as Spurs lost for the second time in a week.

Spurs completed two late deals as the transfer window prepared to slam shut, bringing in French right back Pascal Chimbonda from Wigan and a second Frenchman in the shape of Fulham's skilful and energetic attacking midfielder, Steed Malbranque.

Domestic football then took a backseat for two weeks as players, summoned for international duty by their countries, headed off to participate in Euro 2008 qualifying matches. Berbatov represented Bulgaria in their Group G, 2-2 draw in Romania, but after suffering a groin strain in the match, missed his country's 3-0 victory over Slovakia in Sofia, and returned to Spurs Lodge for treatment.

On his return to the club, Jol expressed his frustration with the situation ahead of the weekend's big clash with Manchester United at Old Trafford: 'Unfortunately, Dimitar got injured in the Bulgaria match. He has come back and cannot play in the next game for his country on Wednesday. He will have treatment here and will hopefully be fit for Saturday's game against Manchester United.'

However, after a week with the physiotherapists in the treatment room, Jol declared to the disappointment of the fans, that Berbatov would miss the United clash: 'Dimitar still has a groin problem and won't be available; hopefully he'll be available next week.'

And without him and Lennon, also injured, Spurs crashed to a third defeat from four despite having chances to take something out of the game. Ryan Giggs headed home the winner to punish Paul Robinson who was only able to parry a free-kick from Ronaldo into his path. The game also saw former Spur Michael Carrick come face-to-face with his former employers for the first time since his departure, while new signings Pascal Chimbonda, Hossam Ghaly and Mido made their debuts for Spurs.

A first trip into European competition for seven long years followed as Spurs, still minus the injured Berbatov, travelled to the Czech Republic to face Slavia Prague in the first round of the UEFA Cup in Prague. A solitary goal from Jermaine Jenas ensured Spurs would take a 1-0 lead into the second leg two weeks later at the Lane, while a frustrating goalless draw at home to Fulham three days later saw Jol's team pick up only their fourth Premier League point out of a possible 15, as Spurs disappointing league form continued. And a heavy 3-0 defeat at Liverpool a week later meant Spurs finished September in a lowly 17th position in the league.

However, a 1-0 second leg victory over Slavia Prague, thanks to Robbie Keane's first goal of the season, sent them into the draw for the group stages of the competition.

Legendary German World Cup winner Paul Breitner gave an exclusive interview to the official match day programme ahead of the Slavia clash and stated his belief that Berbatov, who was still sidelined, possessed the required quality to adapt to the English game and that Spurs would reap the benefits in time: 'A lot of German football fans are interested in Tottenham because Berbatov was very popular there with Leverkusen, a great player and people want to see how he will get on in England.

'I think he will be a key player for Spurs, once he has

got used to the speed of the game and the way you play football here, it is very different to the Bundesliga, where we play at a much slower pace. But once he has played five or 10 games I think he will adapt. It was good for him to score early against Sheffield United, if a new player can score once or twice while they are settling in, that will certainly help them. But they need to come to terms with how their new team-mates are providing chances for them and once they do that, more goals will come, especially for someone as good as Berbatov.'

After missing the five previous matches through injury, Spurs were able to recall the fit-again Berbatov to the starting line up for the early-October visit of Harry Redknapp's Portsmouth. And his inclusion paid immediate dividends, when with just 39 seconds of the match played, Portsmouth keeper David James failed to hold his header to allow Danny Murphy to score his maiden goal for Spurs with a simple back-heeled tap in. A penalty from Defoe doubled their advantage, before ex-Gunner Kanu headed home to reduce the deficit. A first league victory in five games was not to be denied though as Spurs held on to take all three points despite a late push for an equaliser from Pompey.

After the match, goal scorer Murphy told the official website of his admiration for Berbatov: 'He is a clever player and a good athlete – he knows when to come to feet or spin behind. Dimitar has got a calmness and coolness about him that you don't see in many players. It makes him really easy to play alongside. He makes it easy when you get your head up in midfield; he makes the right runs and seems to always make the right decisions.

The sooner he gets back to full match fitness the better because it then gives us great options. Dimitar really does look a terrific player and I think the best has yet to come from him. He has been there and done it, he knows what he's doing – he's scored goals at the top level and you don't do that unless you are a quality player.'

As the players headed off once again on international duty with their respective countries, Jol was left to reflect on the draw for the group stage of the UEFA Cup, after being assigned the challenging task of qualifying for the last 32 from a group containing Besiktas, Club Brugge, Bayer Leverkusen and Dinamo Bucharest.

He said: 'It is a difficult one because we were in the last pot so it was always going to be a hard group. Normally the top three teams would be big favourites, but there are no weaker teams in our group and we will not be viewed as such by the other clubs. It will be an exciting journey for us. Leverkusen is a club with a great history, Dimitar Berbatov played there and they reached the Champions League final in 2002. They will probably be favourites to win the group. Besiktas are not the strongest team in Turkey at the moment but what you are guaranteed over there is a passionate crowd. I think we have done okay, we have Club Brugge at home and if we can get a good result in that it would set us up for the difficult trip to Leverkusen.'

A trip to the Midlands and a tough encounter with Aston Villa faced Spurs as league competition resumed after the international break. With less than 20 minutes of the game remaining, Spurs were reduced to 10 men when Calum Davenport saw red for a last ditch challenge on Gabriel Agbonlahor, only for the Colombian striker Juan Pablo Angel to lash the resulting penalty wide. Minutes later Spurs appeared to have snatched an improbable victory, when Angel's day went from bad to worse as he inadvertently headed Defoe's corner into his own net, only for Gareth Barry to deny them with a marvellous curling finish from long range.

A difficult first-ever trip to Istanbul to face former Fulham manager Jean Tigana's Besiktas and their fanatical support provided Spurs with their first obstacle in Group B of the UEFA Cup. Before the game, Berbatov assessed Spurs' chances of leaving Turkey with a victory, having already assessed the hostile atmosphere at the stadium during his days with Leverkusen: 'The main thing from my own experience with Leverkusen is that we won the game. It was a difficult game and the crowd were very fanatical, they support their team all the way whether they win or lose and they are so loud you cannot hear your team-mate two metres away. I loved it though. That support gives you real power. I think when you have crowds like that it makes you want to play better. Besiktas are a big club and this is a difficult game for us. I've played in Istanbul before, we won that time and we believe we can do it again. We respect them, but we have a number of experienced players here and we have nothing to fear.'

An electric atmosphere in the Inonu Stadium was silenced when Berbatov displayed an exquisite touch to pull down Paul Robinson's long goal kick and fed a delightful pass through for Hossam Ghaly to give the North Londoners the lead at the second time of asking.

Berbatov then wrapped up a well deserved victory in the second half, and sent the travelling supporters into delirium, with a superb solo effort as he burst forward onto Robbie Keane's through ball, turned his marker inside out, and rounded the keeper before rolling the ball into the back of the empty net.

After the impressive win, Jol spoke of his delight at the result and performance: 'We started off well, controlled the first half – that is always important – but we couldn't score more than one goal and that is always difficult against someone like Besiktas. Dimitar Berbatov then showed his extra quality, we scored the second goal at the right moment and then had three or four chances after that.'

Spurs returned to North London high on confidence on the back of their victory in Turkey to face a London derby against a struggling West Ham side at the Lane. Berbatov and his fellow goalscorer in Istanbul, Hossam Ghaly, made way from the team that had started against Besiktas, with Robbie Keane and Danny Murphy also dropping out, as Jol opted to rotate his starting XI. Defoe and Mido replaced Berbatov and Keane up front. It was the Egyptian striker who made his mark on the stroke of half-time in stunning fashion as he flicked up Edgar Davids' low cross and volleyed the ball back across goal and into the bottom of the net for the only goal of the game.

A resounding 5-0 midweek Carling Cup win over Milton Keynes Dons on a wet night at the National Hockey Stadium preceded a disappointing goalless draw away at Watford. Spurs peppered Ben Foster's goal with shots only to find the on-loan keeper in irresistible form for the home team. Spurs finished October positioned in mid-table.

FC Club Brugge of Belgium provided the opposition at the beginning of November, as White Hart Lane played host to Spurs' first UEFA Cup match since their return to European competition. However, the opening exchanges didn't go quite according to plan for Jol's team as Brugge took an unexpected early lead. But, only minutes later, Berbatov rattled home an unstoppable volley from the edge of the area from Pascal Chimbonda's knock down to haul Spurs level. And, despite chances at either end the two sides went into the half-time break all square.

With Spurs dominating the possession as the second half got underway, the Bulgarian international then turned from scorer to provider as his perfectly weighted acrobatic pass, reminiscent of Keane's pass to him for Spurs' second goal against Besiktas, put Keane into acres of space to rifle home an angled drive and put Spurs 2-1 ahead. And, with just under 20 minutes remaining, Berbatov, who had enjoyed a fine game, finished the Belgian team off as he headed home an inviting cross from Ghaly, to cement the team's second win from two games. Ten minutes from full time, Berbatov departed the action to a huge standing ovation from the delighted Lilywhites faithful, with Tottenham's progression from Group B now almost confirmed.

A hugely satisfied Jol spoke after the game of his delight at his team's second half performance, and in particular Berbatov's contribution to the win: 'The second half was probably the best this season. We had flank play, the build-up was good, we kept possession, moved the ball around and we created chances. We could have scored five or six goals and that wasn't easy because Club Brugge dropped off deep. There were some very good performance out there, Lennon was a delight to watch and if Berbatov was good against Besiktas, he was better this time, but I don't want to pick out individuals. Overall I'm a very happy man.'

And a typically modest Berbatov preferred to heap praise on the team as a whole rather than accept the plaudits for a wonderful individual performance, commenting after the game: 'Goals are goals – no matter how you score them. Tonight was a brilliant night for us, we showed a great spirit after going a goal down and we didn't give up and played like a team. Everyone gave 100 per cent and we made it 1-1, 2-1 and then 3-1 to walk away as winners.'

The Bulgarian was equally dismissive of the part he had played in setting up Keane's decisive strike to make the score 2-1: 'Everybody can do that, I saw him and he was alone and I just passed the ball like I do in training. When you train hard and get the opportunity to do things like that in a game, you just do it. For now everything is okay in this competition, but don't forget we have a game in Leverkusen, which will be difficult for us. First though, let's think about the game on Sunday against Chelsea.'

In an interview with the *Daily Telegraph* later that week, Berbatov revealed how he had been settling into his new surroundings and life in general in the capital since his summer transfer from Germany: 'It is too big!

There are only 200,000 people in Leverkusen but here in London there is 40 million or something. I have found my way around though. I go in my car and drive. You have a lot of traffic here. If I want to go into the city I must drive for an hour and 20 minutes. But it's nice. When you get there, there are some beautiful things to see.'

On the subject of football, he revealed that moving to England to play in the Premier League was another forward step in his football education: 'I wanted to come to England because I want to develop. I still have a lot to learn. I can make the most progress here. We are still a young team at Tottenham and I think we have a great future. Last season was great for everybody here and now the expectation is high but I think we have the quality of players to top that.'

On the victory over Brugge, he said: 'I think it was the best performance so far, not only for me but for the club. We did very well, I was very happy, but when you win you usually only look at the good stuff. We must also look at our mistakes so we can correct them next time.'

His father Ivan, he revealed, remains his biggest critic, despite watching most of his son's games from back home in Bulgaria: 'He watched it on the TV. Obviously the good bits are okay but sometimes you must take criticism. He is honest with me. If my dad can't be honest who can? He told me where I must work more to improve myself. I will try to do that.'

The following Sunday's match against reigning Premier League champions Chelsea came at the perfect time for Spurs, with the confidence flowing throughout the whole team. The match would also mark the first time that Berbatov would come face to face in English football with his old team-mate from his time at Leverkusen, Michael Ballack, who had joined the West London club in the summer on a Bosman free transfer from Bayern Munich.

Ahead of the confrontation, Berbatov said: 'He is a top player and it will be a good experience for me to play against him again. I know him well and Chelsea are a top team, but the gaffer will have plans and advice on how we can beat them. They are the champions, but we have a good squad and hopefully we can win on Sunday.'

And win they did, for the first time in league competition for 16 years against their West London rivals on Guy Fawkes night. But it was Chelsea who took the lead. Despite a superb last-ditch tackle from skipper Ledley King to deny Chelsea winger Arjen Robben a likely opening goal, Claude Makelele, who had only scored one goal for the Blues in his three previous seasons at the club, expertly volleyed home from the edge of the area after the resulting corner was only half cleared to him.

After further missed opportunities for Chelsea to extend their lead, Spurs hit back 10 minutes later, when Blues right-back Paulo Ferreira brought down Berbatov out on the left wing, and Michael Dawson rose high above Didier Drogba to head Jermaine Jenas' in-swinging cross past the hapless Hilario in the Chelsea goal, for his first competitive goal in a Spurs shirt.

Keane should have headed Spurs into the lead in the second half when he somehow headed over with the goal at his mercy, before atoning for the miss by dancing past substitute Khalid Boulahrouz on the left wing and crossing to Aaron Lennon. Lennon displayed great composure to control and neatly side foot a volley into the net to send Spurs into the lead and the crowd wild. Despite late chances to equalise and the dismissal of England captain John Terry following an altercation with King, Spurs held on to finally defeat their West London rivals in the league for the first time since 1990 and their first win over them at White Hart Lane since 1987.

The match also marked Martin Jol's second anniversary in charge of the club after inheriting control from Jacques Santini, and the Dutchman was understandably delighted at the full time whistle. He told BBC Sport: 'We needed to win a top game. We tried to attack and be positive. It took 25 minutes to get going but after that we were terrific. It's a long time since we beat Chelsea and it is something to be proud of. They said we'd never beaten a top side and that was a bit annoying but we did that. It was a great performance.'

An extra time 3-1 home win over Port Vale ensured progression to the quarter-finals of the Carling Cup, as the matches continued to come thick and fast for Spurs. Two away trips followed, with the first involving a short journey down the M4 motorway to play Reading at the Madejski. A well dispatched first half penalty from Robbie Keane put Spurs into the lead, after Ghaly was felled in the area after some nice interplay between Berbatov and Keane. Reading hit back soon after though with two quickfire goals before half-time and wrapped up the victory with a third late in the match.

A trip to the north-west to face Mark Hughes' Blackburn team fell on the back of a number of midweek friendly internationals. Berbatov was unable to inspire his Bulgarian colleagues to victory in Slovakia as they lost 3-1 and to further add to his frustration, Jol made the decision to rest him against Blackburn until the final few minutes of the 1-1 draw at Ewood. With a huge and potentially decisive UEFA Cup match against Berbatov's former club Bayer Leverkusen scheduled just days after the Blackburn game, it appeared Jol was saving his star striker for an emotional return to the BayArena.

Ahead of the journey to face his former friends and team-mates, Berbatov told the *Daily Mail* how he felt about the draw which pitted Spurs against the club he was idolised at for five-and-a-half years, and his expectations for the game:

'I was at home when they told me we had drawn Bayer Leverkusen because I was on international duty. I was sick. I had five wonderful years there but that is over. It will be strange, but I am a professional player. I play for Tottenham and I will try to score. It doesn't matter that they are my friends; I will forget about that and try to help my team. I will celebrate like usual, raise my hand and show that I have scored. I appreciate that I play for Tottenham and I will try to show that with my goals.'

He also revealed his reaction to being brought on in the 2002 Champions League final, and how far he felt Spurs could progress in the UEFA Cup: 'I was so young that I didn't give a damn. I was sitting on the bench and thinking nothing. Then the coach said you are in and I was like "OK, whatever". Maybe when time goes by I will appreciate that it might never happen again. But the Tottenham team is a mix of youth and experience and, hopefully, we can achieve something as big as that. I think we have the quality to win the UEFA Cup. Tottenham have perhaps seen the best of me in this competition. I know about that and I am working as hard as possible to improve my quality in England.'

Meanwhile, Leverkusen coach Michael Skibbe revealed on the eve of the game, the high regard that Berbatov was still held in, back in Germany: 'We miss him very much here in Leverkusen. He's one of the best strikers in the world. He's got wonderful technique, is good with his head, both feet are fast and all the time he has an eye for players in better positions. He's special. It's his first season in England, so in six, eight or 10 months he will be special and grow more and more. I'm sure he will be one of the best players in the Premiership.'

In a game of spurned opportunities, inevitably perhaps, it was Berbatov who struck the winning goal against his former team, as he tapped home from close range Aaron Lennon's centre after the winger had been put clear by a lovely slide rule pass from Keane. Spurs and Berbatov were guilty of passing up further opportunities to increase the advantage, but their frugality in front of goal didn't return to haunt them as they held on to make it three wins from three group games, and in turn ensure qualification for the knock out stages of the competition.

Jol was quick to express his delight at the win and in particular offered worthy praise to his goalscoring hero of the night: 'Every time we play in Europe he is outstanding. In the league he's not there yet but he has all the talent – we are pretty confident he will be the same player he was in Germany for his last two or three seasons. He played for Leverkusen for five years and was a young guy when he came over, so he was a bit sensitive about this game. He said Juan [Leverkusen's Brazilian defender] knew him very well so I said maybe he could come up with some new tricks. The only thing was he could have scored a couple more – this was a night for four or five goals.'

As usual, Berbatov remained unruffled by his winning goal and the praise being directed his way, preferring instead to divert the praise onto the team: 'It was hard for the team and harder for me. I am happy to have scored, we won and now we are in the second phase. That is what we wanted and we have achieved it. I try to do my best and score goals but it is not about me, it is about the whole squad. We are working hard and now we must think about the Premiership and Wigan at home on Sunday. It was special, I was here for almost six years and it was very flattering to have the crowd chanting my name. That is why I didn't over-celebrate when I scored out of respect for the people here. I was happy to score though. It is hard for players when they come up against their former club and I am no exception. I am happy to have done my job and we've got the points.'

After the euphoria of their European progress, the team returned to Premier League action with the visit of Wigan to the Lane. After going behind to a Henri Camara strike, Spurs hit back with two of their own in the space of two minutes to take a 2-1 lead into the half-time interval. The first came courtesy of a wonderful piece of skill from Jermaine Defoe, who bamboozled his marker to spin and crash a left foot shot into the roof of the net, after being put through by Berbatov, who had himself shown impressive strength and vision to put his strike partner in on goal. Defoe's strike was his 50th goal in the Premier League and came in his 100th league appearance for Spurs.

Barely a minute later, Spurs doubled their advantage as Berbatov engineered himself a goal of equal quality to Defoe's, nutmegging Wigan defender Matt Jackson before clinically curling a rising shot into the top corner of the net, for his second goal of the league campaign thus far. And, with only seconds remaining, after being set free down the left wing, Berbatov capped another fine individual performance by coolly picking out Lennon for the clincher. The match was Spurs' 200th Premier League victory.

Once again, after the final whistle, Jol felt compelled to applaud Berbatov's contribution to the game: 'The crowd was good, lifted us again and we scored another through Dimitar Berbatov. It was a great goal that had nothing to do with team play as he did it out of nothing.'

December was welcomed by the short and highly anticipated journey to face bitter rivals Arsenal at the new Emirates Stadium, but it proved a forgettable day for the Lilywhites faithful and the team as the first North London derby of the season and 152nd in total ended in a 3-0 defeat for Spurs. Steed Malbranque might have given Spurs an early lead after being set up by Berbatov, before Adebayor opened the scoring for the Gunners.

A highly contentious penalty, awarded by referee

Graham Poll despite Spurs defender Pascal Chimbonda getting a foot to the ball as Tomas Rosicky closed in on goal, was converted by Arsenal captain Gilberto Silva to give the home team a 2-0 lead at the break. And Poll awarded a second dubious penalty kick of the day to Arsenal with just under 20 minutes of the match remaining. Robin van Persie clearly handled the ball before falling under the close attentions of Jermaine Jenas, who to his amazement was penalised for a foul. Gilberto stroked home the resulting penalty for his second of the day to complete a thoroughly miserable day for the visitors, who would have to wait until the end of January for a chance to reclaim the bragging rights in North London.

Spurs bounced back from their derby disappointment with a home victory over Middlesbrough – the first of five in a row – thanks to a stunning late long-range winner from Robbie Keane. Minutes earlier an equaliser from Robert Huth appeared to have denied Spurs the victory, after they had taken the lead through another superb goal from Berbatov. The Bulgarian, who had begun to produce the sort of form in the league that had prompted Jol to sign him in the summer, swivelled on a header across goal from Chimbonda and thumped the ball home high into the net with a tremendous volley.

A medial knee ligament injury towards the end of the Boro game would confine Keane to the treatment table for the next six weeks, but Spurs, with Berbatov beginning to find form, didn't appear to miss him as they rattled five goals past Les Reed's struggling Charlton team at the Lane. Berbatov opened the scoring with a cool toe-poked finish before Teemu Tainio's deflected shot put them two up in the first half. Although Charlton pulled a goal back before half-time, Spurs regained their two goal advantage after the break as Steed Malbranque scored his first goal for the club from Berbatov's measured knock down and added to their lead when Defoe smashed home the fourth. Berbatov rounded off the destruction with a powerful left footed strike, his second of the game and ninth of the season.

After another virtuoso performance from the Bulgarian, Jol told the official club website: 'I have to say Dimitar Berbatov is now someone who is looking extremely dangerous.'

After taking time to settle into his new club and the rigours of the Premier League, Berbatov was now beginning to show the supporters why Jol had been so eager to splash out such a big fee to secure his signature in the summer. With the goals now starting to flow, Berbatov told the *London Evening Standard* of his determination to do well for the club and to score the goals that would bring success in the form of silverware to White Hart Lane for the first time since 1999.

'I am aware that Tottenham have had great strikers in the past who left their mark here. I want to do the same. Jurgen [Klinsmann] was a big hit here, he scored a lot of goals and he was a great striker. I am just starting and I have my own style. I want to be the next Tottenham striker to get 20 league goals and I aim to do it this season. It will be great for me and the club. Our goal is to be in the top four in the table and my goals could get us there. I know Jurgen was very popular with the fans.

Many fans wore shirts with his name on the back and the kids loved him. But I feel we have a great relationship already. Maybe, one day, some kids will want to be me.'

Berbatov also revealed in the interview how he likens football to art: 'Football is like art and I am sometimes trying to do a masterpiece. I feel some of my goals this season have been masterpieces, although I am happy with any goal.'

And he admitted that his father was a major influence on his career and someone who he always looks to for advice: 'We have a very close relationship. I talk to him all the time. He is my friend and I speak with him after every game. I'm not an arrogant player because I know it is not an individual sport like tennis. It's a team effort. It is something my father taught me. He told me to always keep my feet on the ground and I try and do that no matter how well I am playing or how many goals I score. He always tells me when I don't do something right and I make an extra effort to do better next time.

'I trust him because he used to be a player himself. He started out as a striker but then went on to be a defender, so he has the best advice as he knows what it's like to be trying to score goals and stop them. As a striker it's good to know what defenders will try and do before they can do it. I feel I am one step ahead of them. He hasn't been able to come over to see me play but I hope that will change next year when Bulgaria becomes part of the European Union and there won't be a visa issue.'

Berbatov continued: 'I think we have what it takes to win the UEFA Cup. I think we have surprised people across Europe with our results and the way we have played. I was at Leverkusen when they got to the Champions League final in 2002 and I see Tottenham's squad has similar qualities.'

After trouncing Charlton, Spurs looked forward to the chance to record a fourth consecutive win in the UEFA Cup as they welcomed Romanian outfit Dinamo Bucharest to North London. And a 3-1 victory duly wrapped up top spot in the group and a place in the last 32. Berbatov had opened the scoring when he hammered home a long range shot after Dinamo's goalkeeper gifted him possession, before two goals from Defoe sealed the victory.

The draw for the first knock out stage followed later that week and paired Spurs with their 1974 UEFA Cup final opponents Feyenoord. However, unlike in 1974, when Spurs lost the second leg 2-0 in Rotterdam, and 4-2 on aggregate to the Dutch team, Spurs would enjoy the advantage of playing the second leg at home. And a tie against SC Braga of Portugal or Parma of Italy would await the winners.

A difficult trip north to face Manchester City at Eastlands ensured European aspirations were put to one side for the time being, as Spurs sought to present Jol with a win in his 100th game in charge of the club. Goals from Calum Davenport and a spectacular strike from Tom Huddlestone did just that, as Spurs won on the road for the first time all season.

Substitute Berbatov provided the inspiration for an extra time victory over Southend in the quarter-finals of the Carling Cup to set up a mouth-watering clash with bitter rivals Arsenal in the semi-finals. Before the game,

Defoe spoke once again in the match day programme of his enjoyment at playing alongside Berbatov: 'Berba is such a silky player. He's got a great touch and we've linked up really well. I've enjoyed playing alongside him, he shows good movement and is on fire at the moment. You can really make a pairing work when you get a few games together. I think we've got a little understanding and it is showing.'

But Spurs' run of five straight victories ended in the very next game as Newcastle ran out 3-1 winners in the league encounter at St. James' Park two days before Christmas.

Jol's team bounced back though with a 2-1 Boxing Day win over Aston Villa at the Lane as Defoe notched another two goals and Berbatov provided another two assists. Despite a closely fought 1-0 loss to Liverpool in driving rain and swirling wins at the Lane, which ended a run of 12 home wins in a row in all competitions, Spurs would begin 2007 in eighth position in the league with qualification for European football the next season still a real very realistic possibility. After the defeat, Jol praised Berbatov's dedication to the Spurs cause, as the striker made himself available to sit on the substitute's bench despite illness.

'Dimitar Berbatov was ill and had nearly a 40 degrees temperature. Mido couldn't play yesterday [Friday] but I said to him he would have to play and he's a good lad, he did a final test before the game and was 80, 90 per cent fit. I spoke to Berbatov this morning [Saturday] and asked if he felt better and could sit on the bench, he said yes and maybe he could play for 10 minutes but in the end it was a bit more and I felt he did unbelievably well, on Friday he was in bed with a fever. I feel Berbatov will be fine for Portsmouth on Monday.'

Berbatov was indeed fit for the New Year's Day trip to the south coast and it was he who started the move that rescued a point for Spurs at Fratton Park as Malbranque's header equalised Benjani's opener for Portsmouth. With the January transfer window open again for one month, Jol moved to strengthen the squad with the signings of goalkeeper Ben Alnwick from Sunderland as backup to Paul Robinson, and Adel Taarabt on loan from French outfit RC Lens. A tricky looking tie against Cardiff in South Wales yielded a 0-0 draw in the third round of the FA Cup, with Robbie Keane boosting Spurs by returning to action after recovering from the knee injury which had kept him out for eight matches. A replay would be necessary 10 days later at the Lane to separate the two teams.

Meanwhile, assuming Spurs could overcome the Bluebirds in the replay, the fourth round draw saw them paired with either Barnsley or Southend, after the two teams also drew their third round match. Fans of Tottenham received a belated Christmas present the day after the drawn match in Cardiff, as exciting star winger Aaron Lennon committed himself to the club long term by penning a five-and-a-half-year contract to remain at the Lane. In addition, there was more good news on the injury front with captain Ledley King close to a return to action after missing three matches with a foot injury.

Tottenham's first home Premier League match of 2007 saw them welcome Newcastle to the Lane, but it turned out to be a disappointing day for the home support as the

Geordies somehow returned to the north-east with a second win over the Lilywhites in three weeks. Defoe had given Spurs an early lead, only for Newcastle to equalise within two minutes. Berbatov volleyed home his 11th goal of the season and first in seven games to restore the advantage in the second half, before two goals in the space of two minutes from Obafemi Martins and Nicky Butt, and Shay Given's heroics in the Newcastle goal, secured Glenn Roeder's men a much-needed win and all three points.

Spurs had little time to lick their wounds, however. Three days later Cardiff travelled to White Hart Lane for the cup replay confident of causing an upset, but Spurs were in no mood to oblige them as they romped to a stunning 4-0 victory. The following day UEFA announced that Feyenoord, who had been drawn to face Spurs in the next round of the UEFA Cup, had been excluded from European competition due to crowd violence during their European away match with Nancy. The only unresolved matter would be whether Spurs would gain a bye into the next round or not, to be decided by UEFA at a later date.

A 1-1 draw with London neighbours Fulham served as a warm up to the potentially explosive midweek first leg Carling Cup semi-final with North London rivals Arsenal. And explosive it was. Before the game, the fans were introduced to Jol's new signing, defender Ricardo Rocha after kick-off was delayed by 15 minutes. But when the match did get underway, it did so at a typically frenzied pace for a North London derby.

Berbatov came closest to opening the scoring in the

early minutes as he displayed exquisite control to fashion a shot, which struck the outside of Manuel Almunia's near post. He didn't have to wait long for a goal though, as he rose unmarked to head home a teasing cross from Lennon. However, Spurs' chances were dealt a blow when Berbatov was forced off, after sustaining a groin injury in the process of scoring the opening goal.

Nevertheless, the team further boosted their fans' dreams of a first cup final since 1999, when Arsenal's Julio Baptista deflected Tom Huddlestone's dangerous free-kick past his own goalkeeper to put Spurs 2-0 ahead shortly afterwards. But, two second half goals from Baptista, at the right end this time, levelled the tie for Arsenal. Then Almunia denied Defoe to clinch the Gunners a draw from the jaws of defeat.

Jol was understandably upset with the final score after seeing his side squander a commanding 2-0 advantage: 'We're all very disappointed because we were 2-0 up, but we've only got ourselves to blame. I have to be honest, the first 25 minutes was outstanding and a lot of that had to do with Dimitar Berbatov because he can hold up the ball, play himself or go into the spaces. It didn't help that he had to go off but it was still 2-0 to us. Berbatov's problem was his groin. He scored and then came to the touchline and told us he had a minor problem. Hopefully he won't be out for too long.'

The next day brought good news for Spurs' fixture calendar, when UEFA announced that the club would receive a bye into the last 16 of the UEFA Cup, following Feyenoord's exclusion from the competition for crowd misbehaviour. Meanwhile, Berbatov's injury ruled him out of the 3-1 FA Cup win over Southend, as Spurs secured a fifth round tie with Fulham. With only two days of the transfer window remaining Spurs bode a fond farewell to bullish Dutch midfielder Edgar Davids, who departed for Ajax after 18 months at the club.

With Berbatov still sidelined by the groin injury he picked up in the Carling Cup first leg, his absence was sorely felt as Spurs capitulated to a 3-1 defeat in the second leg of the Carling Cup semi-final at the Emirates. They lost the tie 5-3 on aggregate to leave the fans' dreams of getting to a cup final resting upon FA and UEFA Cup progression.

The team entered February lying 10th in the league and well positioned to challenge for a European place. But, despite having Berbatov back from injury, the month got off to a dreadful start with Manchester United claiming a convincing 4-0 victory at the Lane. The team's Carling Cup hangover appeared to be lingering.

A number of first team players received call-ups by their respective national team managers after the United match. Berbatov represented Bulgaria in the final of a four-team international tournament against Cyprus, and scored twice to take his international tally to an astounding 33 goals in just 57 games. In scoring his two goals it moved him to within four of his coach at international level, Hristo Stoichkov's own number.

Back in the Premier League, results didn't improve for the team as they went down 2-1 at Bramall Lane, after taking an early lead, to a Sheffield United team battling desperately against relegation after just a season back in the Premier League. Once again, it was left to the team's cup form to provide respite from Premier League struggles as Fulham were bowled over 4-0 in the FA Cup fifth round at Craven Cottage. Robbie Keane put Spurs in control of the tie with two superb volleys before Berbatov, who had only been introduced to the action four minutes earlier, joined in the party by side footing home after his initial shot had rebounded to him off the post. Amazingly it was his first away goal for the team on English soil. And, it was the classy Bulgarian who completed the scoring with a cute chip over the goalkeeper to set up an intriguing quarter-final with double league champions, Chelsea.

A tough game against Everton at Goodison awaited with the two teams vying for European qualification by virtue of their league position. Spurs had yet to win a league game in 2007, but Berbatov set them on the way to rectifying that, when he confidently swept home a cross from Lennon to put them into the lead. Mikel Arteta's delightful free-kick brought the scores level at half-time, but Jermaine Jenas secured a vital three points for Spurs in the last minute of the match with an accurate curling shot from outside the area.

With their first victory of the year achieved, Spurs hoped to add the scalp of high-flying Bolton to Everton's as the Lancashire side travelled down to London with the race for European places hotting up. Ahead of the match, Berbatov reminisced about his debut for Spurs in the 2-0 loss against the same opposition in August 2006: 'It was my first game in England and it was hard for me. Bolton are a physical team, but now they are coming to White Hart Lane and a long time has passed since my first game. Things are different now. We play at home and have a great chance to win, but we know it will be difficult.'

And win they did, and comfortably so despite having Keane sent off after 37 minutes for handling on the line to prevent a certain goal for Bolton. Keane had already grabbed to two goals to help Spurs into a 3-0 lead before receiving his marching orders, at which point Spurs were forced to play with Berbatov as a lone front man. Bolton scored the resulting penalty but the Bulgarian showed fantastic commitment to the Spurs cause to keep the pressure on the opposition, before displaying wonderful close control and awareness to set up Lennon for a fourth to wrap up a second consecutive win.

Delighted with his star striker's attitude and commitment after Keane's dismissal, Jol issued lavish praise on Berbatov after the final whistle to the Spurs website: 'We broke on them three or four times and could have scored more goals in the second half and I told Berbatov that it was probably the best performance I've seen from a striker on his own against any team.

'It's always a worry [for a foreign player coming into the Premiership] if he can do it in the first couple of months but, especially at White Hart Lane, he was immaculate. The thing that pleased me most is that he took responsibility. He wants to do well for us, he knows how much I wanted him as a player and he wants to do well for me and the club, and that's great. Berbatov could play for any team in Europe because he's a top-class player. Just look at his international record – I don't think anyone can better his goal scoring record for Bulgaria.'

Spurs and England midfielder, Jermaine Jenas, also voiced his admiration for his team-mate's work ethic during the game: 'We had to stand up and be counted, all of us, and I thought Dimitar up front was exceptional. The sort of quality and professionalism he displayed in attack carried right throughout the team.'

And the praise kept coming as Spurs legend and development coach, Clive Allen described Berbatov's performance against Bolton as sensational: 'I thought it was a sensational performance. It's certainly the best he's given us this season and showed what he's capable of. He held the ball up superbly well, at times he was isolated with two or three defenders around him but he showed clever movement and unbelievable touch, he was completely in control of the ball and therefore was able to link up when we were short of numbers. It was a wonderful display. He's been linking well with Robbie, Mido's done well when he's been introduced and what you have is healthy competition for places. Everyone is keen to play and score goals and that's exactly how you want it.'

Spurs ended February in ninth position in the Premier League and a 4-3 victory in an amazing London derby, away at struggling West Ham, kept their good run of league form going. With the score at 3-2 in favour of the Hammers with just five minutes of the match remaining, Berbatov curled home a perfect free-kick from the edge of the area to draw the sides level. Then Paul Stalteri sealed a dramatic win with virtually the last kick of the match, as West Ham went all-out for victory in their battle to avoid the drop.

Martin Jol was typically overjoyed with the late win, and also spoke of Berbatov's almost obligatory contribution to the victory: 'It was like hell, heaven, hell and heaven. It was an amazing English game. Berbatov struck his free-kick very well to bring the scores level at 3-3 but, as is often said in England, one swallow doesn't make a summer, so we will have to see how he gets on from a free-kick next time. He mentioned it to me a little while ago, suggesting he was a specialist from his younger days in Sofia. This was an opportunity for him and maybe we will now use him more in those situations in the future.'

The following Thursday saw Spurs travel to Portugal for a UEFA Cup match with Braga, who had overcome Parma in the previous round, and the Londoners returned home triumphantly with three important away goals to take into the second leg in a 3-2 win.

Goals were coming thick and fast for Spurs now, both for and against and the pattern didn't alter when the team came up against Chelsea in the FA Cup quarter-final showdown at Stamford Bridge. Berbatov smashed Spurs into the lead after being put through by Lennon, before Frank Lampard equalised, only for Spurs to take a 3-1 lead in at half-time thanks to an own goal from Michael Essien and a strike from Hossam Ghaly. However, Chelsea were not to be denied as Lampard notched his second of the afternoon and Salomon Kalou volleyed home a late leveller. Although it was only the width of a crossbar that denied Spurs a famous win late on as Defoe's shot cannoned back off the woodwork.

Although disappointed with not holding out for

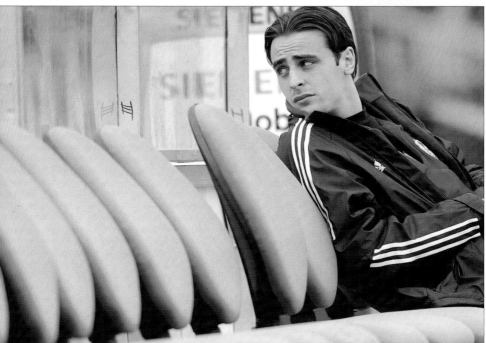

Above: Berbatov (*standing, far left*) and his Leverkusen teammates after losing the 2002 Champions League final 2-1 to Real Madrid.

Below: On the bench during a match with Bayern Munich in 2003.

Representing Bulgaria against Denmark at Euro 2004 in Portugal.

Above: Marco Materazzi fouls Berbatov in the Bulgaria v Italy match during Euro 2004.

Below: Dimitar Berbatov scores a penalty past Frank Rost when Leverkusen played Schalke in September 2005.

Above: Disbelief at missing an easy chance during Leverkusen v Arminia Bielefeld in October 2005.

Inset: At Spurs in November 2006, substituted while playing against his former team-mates at Leverkusen.

Above: Celebrating his second goal against Luxembourg during the Bulgarian Euro 2008 Group G qualifying football match in September 2007.

Inset: Berbatov with Robbie Keane, the team-mate with whom he formed such a prolific partnership at Spurs.

Below: More celebrations after helping Spurs claim the Carling Cup with a 2-1 win over Chelsea at Wembley in February 2008.

Above: Presented to the media by Sir Alex after completing his dream move to United in September 2008.

Below: Manchester United 2008/09: (*back left to right*) Edwin Van Der Sar, Nemanja Vidic, John O'Shea, Rio Ferdinand, Dimitar Berbatov, Cristiano Ronaldo and (*front row left to right*) Paul Scholes, Wayne Rooney, Patrice Evra, Michael Carrick and Ryan Giggs.

Dream triumvirate: Berbatov, Tevez and Ronaldo celebrate another goal against
West Ham on 29 October 2008.

Above: Playing Celtic in October 2008 in a Champions League match.

Below: Philippe Senderos, *left*, and Bulgarian captain Berbatov during a friendly match against Switzerland in February 2009.

victory at Stamford Bridge, Spurs had to raise themselves for the second leg of the UEFA Cup against Braga the following Thursday. Before the match, the long-serving first team coach, Chris Hughton, gave his verdict to the club website on Berbatov's contribution to the team thus far during the season:

'Dimitar is a quality, classy footballer. Perhaps if people hadn't taken much notice of him before, they certainly did after the Bolton game where he played up front by himself for a large part of the game. Where his qualities are is the way he can manoeuvre the ball and his feel for it, plus his runs. He is somebody that does it at his own pace, he is not lightening quick, but when he runs with the ball he has got the ability to go past people.'

Houghton continued: 'You see the times when he runs close to the touchline, he has such good awareness of the players around him that he is able to keep hold of it. He has certainly got better and better and stronger and stronger as the season has gone on. I think where we are fortunate with Berba is that he is not a young, raw player. He is one who has been around for a while with a lot of experience from playing in a tough league for a good number of seasons.

'We've got him at a good age, although it does take time to adapt to English football because it is a different game. The quality has always been there though. I remember his first few training sessions and you do get a feel for a player when he arrives and you see him first hand for the first time. My first thoughts were "he is certainly a good footballer, how is he going to show that week to week?" He has definitely got better as the season has gone on in that respect.'

And it was another inspired performance from Berbatov that put Spurs through to the last eight of the UEFA Cup as he struck twice and set up another to secure a 3-2 victory. After going 1-0 down, Berbatov finished calmly from Keane's through-ball to put Spurs back in front on aggregate before displaying exquisite control to chest down Tom Huddlestone's long pass and hammer home a volley to put Spurs 2-1 up on the night. Although Braga showed resolute spirit to equalise, Berbatov set up the winning goal for Malbranque as he deftly clipped a ball with the outside of his foot into the Frenchman's path. An enthralling tie with reigning UEFA Cup holders Sevilla was assured.

Jol was once again left with little option other than to praise his in-form striker after a virtuoso performance: 'Dimitar set up the first goal with a one-two with Robbie Keane, the second goal was a great goal and he set up the third goal with a one-two with Steed Malbranque, so I'm very happy with him.'

Berbatov remained on the bench for the 3-1 victory over Watford at the Lane, Jol holding the Bulgarian back for the cup replay with Chelsea three days later. However, it proved to be a disappointing night for Spurs and their fans with Robbie Keane's penalty proving in vain as stunning goals from Andriy Shevchenko and Shaun Wright-Phillips put the Blues into the semi-finals of the cup.

Spurs finished March in eighth place in the league and started April well with a fifth consecutive victory in the

Premier League over Reading, getting a first clean sheet since October in the process. A testing midweek trip to Andalusia to face championship-chasing Sevilla followed in the first leg of the UEFA Cup quarter-final, and in the run-up to the match, Berbatov and the club received a boost as the former Leverkusen striker deservedly scooped the March award for the PFA Barclays Premier League Fans' Player of the Month.

Although Keane gave the travelling hordes of fans plenty to cheer early on, after latching onto Berbatov's ball to put Spurs 1-0 up with just two minutes played, Spurs headed back to London disappointed and a goal behind after Sevilla were awarded a highly dubious penalty which former Spur Freddie Kanoute dispatched, and Alexander Kerzhakov headed home the winner.

Less than 48 hours later Spurs travelled to Stamford Bridge to face Chelsea. A 1-0 loss ended the team's run of five straight Premier League victories ahead of the return clash with Sevilla at the Lane. Despite a crackling atmosphere at White Hart Lane, it was Sevilla who broke the deadlock as Steed Malbranque unluckily sliced a flicked corner into his own net with just three minutes gone. And Kanoute virtually ended the tie five minutes later when he sliced through the defence to put the Andalusian side 4-1 up on aggregate. Goals from Defoe and Lennon cut the deficit but for Spurs and their loyal fans, the hunt for trophies had come to an earlier than expected end.

Back in the Premier League the goals kept flowing as Spurs came from behind three times to salvage a 3-3 draw in a thrilling game away at Wigan. Berbatov

141

grabbed his 20th of the season with a lovely finish and Keane added a brace to give Spurs a share of the spoils as the team and fans geared up ahead of the season's big home derby match against Arsenal. And it was Keane once more who sent the home fans wild at the Lane, when he stooped to nod in Michael Dawson's flick from a corner, to give Spurs a 1-0 lead at half-time in the derby. However, goals from the unmarked Kolo Toure and Emmanuel Adebayor appeared to have won the game and a league double over Spurs for Arsenal, until a rasping long range effort from Jenas ensured a share of the spoils for both North London teams.

The day after the derby match, Berbatov received a personal accolade to be proud of as he was only one of three players not from Manchester United – the others being Liverpool captain Steven Gerrard and Chelsea's Didier Drogba – to be included in the PFA's Team of the Year in his debut season at Spurs. Damien Comolli, Tottenham's sporting director, said of the honour: 'I'm pleased the fans can watch a player like him play week in, week out and his attitude and commitment has been tremendous. He's a winner and he passes that to the other players.'

Chris Hughton concurred with Comolli's sentiments, adding: 'Berba's one of those players that other professionals will look at and, one, appreciate his value to the team, his hold-up skills and ability to score goals and two, I'm sure they would also marvel at some of his wonderful touches.

'He can, at any given time of the game, do something other players can't do and that certainly excites fellow professionals. Manchester United have a big presence in the team and generally, it is selected from players in the top four teams and then a team outside of that who are seen to have a good season – a player who has contributed to that has a chance to get in. Probably the most satisfying thing for us and Berba is the quality of players around and anyone who gets in that team can look at the players in his position and be delighted that they've got in front of those players.'

And Bayern Munich midfielder Owen Hargreaves, a former opponent during the Bulgarian's time at Leverkusen, also reserved special words of praise for Berbatov in the *Daily Mail*: 'This season Berbatov has been a breath of fresh air in English football, he just makes the game look so easy at times. I'm not surprised by how well he has done because he has always been a great footballer. He was impressive in Germany but he never really showed his class on a consistent game-by-game basis. The transfer to Tottenham has been fantastic for him because he has been forced to take his game on to a completely different level.'

Meanwhile, a delighted Berbatov told the club's website of his happiness at making the team: 'It is a big honour. I was very pleased and very happy when I found out about it, especially as it comes from my fellow players. I wouldn't have done it without the help of my team-mates and hopefully in the future I will continue to play like this. Manchester United deserve it. Those players have played so well all season and Drogba and Gerrard are the same. To tell you the truth, I was surprised to be in there, but very happy and very honoured.'

He continued: 'The most important thing is that the team is doing well. From the first day everyone was really nice to me, not only the guys in the team, but all the people who work around the team too. It really helped me to settle and I am really thankful for that. The way to show that I'm really thankful is to score goals and to play the way I can.'

With the season drawing to a close and European qualification a must, Berbatov spoke to the website about the impending clash with Middlesbrough at the Riverside and a reunion with a familiar face, former Leverkusen team-mate Emanuel Pogatetz: 'He's a tough defender and he's a little crazy, but you have to be crazy to be a defender. He's a great guy and I had a great time with him during my time at Bayer Leverkusen, when we were together for four seasons. He's very young, younger than me and he's doing well for Middlesbrough, so I'm pleased for him and it will be difficult for us.'

However, Berbatov also revealed that although he was looking forward to seeing his friend again, he doesn't particularly like playing against former team-mates: 'Sometimes it's difficult. Personally, I don't like it too much, but once you step on the pitch there are no friends – you play for your team and try to win the game.'

And Berbatov's policy showed as he shrugged off Pogatetz's challenge to set up Keane for the opening goal of the game. The three-time Bulgarian Footballer of the Year then put the stamp on his quality as he acrobatically volleyed home a Hossam Ghaly cross to put Spurs 2-0 up. Although Boro pulled a goal back, Keane's second wrapped up the points late on before Berbatov's friend Pogatetz headed home a late consolation.

After the win, which put Spurs eighth in the table with a game in hand over the sides above them, Berbatov's team-mates appeared to queue up to marvel at his wonder strike. Goalkeeper Paul Robinson said, tongue-in-cheek: 'Berba's strike was half-decent. The ball came over to him and I was thinking "what's he doing? Don't hit that", but it turned out to be a great goal.'

Strike partner Keane, who broke the 20-goal barrier himself during the match, added: 'Berba has been tremendous this season. Considering it is his first one in the Premiership he has taken to it no problem and it shows in his performances. He scored a great goal from a good ball from Hossam Ghaly. I was right behind it and was lucky to see it fly in – he has been doing that sort of thing all season.'

And central defender Michael Dawson also paid homage, adding: 'We're exciting at the moment. We're scoring goals, but conceding goals and the players we've got keep pulling us out of trouble – fantastic goals from Keano and Berba again, Berba's was amazing.'

The day before the season's final away game at Charlton, the in-form Berbatov and Keane received the joint honour of Barclays Player of the Month for April after the strike partners helped themselves to eight goals in five Premier League games that month.

Berbatov helped himself to another fantastic goal against Charlton as his deft touch from Ledley King's long ball took him past the last defender to coolly finish past on-loan goalkeeper Scott Carson. Defoe's late strike from Berbatov's through pass clinched a 2-0 victory and condemned his former club to relegation to the

Championship, while keeping Spurs firmly in the hunt for a UEFA Cup place.

Blackburn provided the opposition in the penultimate game of the season at the Lane, as Spurs ended any hopes Rovers had left of qualifying for the UEFA Cup, despite going 1-0 behind to Benni McCarthy's first half header. However, when Rovers' goalkeeper Brad Friedel could only parry Berbatov's low shot midway through the second half, Defoe was on hand to put away the rebound to earn a point for Spurs, which meant a draw at home against Manchester City in their final game of the season would be enough to ensure European football the following season.

In the final match programme of the season, Berbatov revealed his thoughts on his increasing status as a hero at the Lane, saying: 'Becoming a hero is not what I am about, I am just a normal guy trying to enjoy my time here and trying to entertain the fans – that is the most important thing for me. If I can do that I will be happy.'

Goals from the clinical duo of Keane and Berbatov wrapped up a 2-1 victory and UEFA Cup qualification in the process as the team finished the season on a high note. Martin Jol expressed his delight after the match at the team's durability and determination to finish the season well and clinch fifth spot for the second season in a row: 'It means the world to us to finish fifth again. We knew we were in a fine position a couple of weeks ago. Although people were saying we had a slight chance, we had two games in hand and we knew we were on a good run. In fact, the only game we lost in the final spell was against Chelsea when we had to play 32 hours after playing in Seville. We normally got a result after a European match, but not this time.

'It wasn't easy though', he continued. 'We were the only team to play three games in six days this week and that showed in the second half. But we showed a lot of resilience and character and there were a few heroes out there. Of course, I was happy to see Dimitar and Robbie score the goals again, but I'm very proud of them all.'

With a successful season complete and having stolen the show with his repertoire of magical skills and great goals, Berbatov was deservedly named Club Member's Player of the Season. However, although content with his first season at the club he declared that he hoped to help Spurs win trophies, saying: 'I want to win something with Tottenham and I think we can do it.'

And in an interview with the official Spurs programme he revealed how much he had enjoyed his first season in English football, and also how much he had appreciated the support of Spurs' loyal supporters and his colleagues at the club:

'It is enjoyable, fast, has physical contact, great players, great teams and the fans are so passionate here in England – it is unbelievable. It gives you everything you want in order to produce your best football. I think the fans are more passionate about football than in Germany because the game was born here. They live for their football and when you don't have a break in the winter and keep playing, it is for the fans and to entertain them. The people love football and cannot live without it. I will play and play and not complain, as long as the fans are happy with my game and with the team then there will be no problems.

'Against Southend, for example, when I went to warm up and the fans were singing my name it was a precious moment for me. It showed me that I must be doing my job and I will work more and more to improve myself and make them happy. On the night it was so cold, but they were there supporting us for the whole 120 minutes. It didn't matter that we were playing against a Championship team, they were with us just the same as usual.'

Berbatov continued: 'I say it all the time, it was because of the guys in the team [that I was able to fit in so quickly] who welcomed me straight away – this is the main reason. When you go to a different country and you go into a squad where you don't know anybody, of course, you will be nervous. But you see how the guys treat you and welcome you, you calm down and are able to play your game.

'It doesn't matter if you come from Germany, Italy, Spain or Bulgaria, you are coming into what I feel is the best league in the world and you must quickly get used to the pace of the game, the tackles and the passion of the fans. It is good to know the language, it helped me a lot being able to communicate with the players from the beginning. If you want to succeed, you must keep training, work hard and then you will not fail.'

CHAPTER 9

EARLY SECOND SEASON BLUES

'If you don't win anything, you have had a bad season.'
BILL NICHOLSON

For the second season in succession, Spurs boss Martin Jol – who had signed Berbatov before the end of May in 2006 – began his pre-season shopping well before the start of the 2007–08 campaign, when he beat a number of interested parties to the signing of Southampton's highly-rated teenage left-back Gareth Bale. The Welsh international signed for a fee believed to be worth up to a possible £10 million in May and again highlighted Jol's liking for securing the cream of English football's young talent. Upon signing, the free-kick expert told the official website: 'I am just excited to be coming to a big club, a massive club like Tottenham. I want to play in the Premiership, Tottenham is a club pushing forward and I want to be part of its future.'

Meanwhile, reacting to widespread speculation in the media at the start of June that a number of clubs could be considering a move for star striker, Berbatov and Spurs' other top stars, sporting director Damien Comolli said: 'It is unbelievable picking up a newspaper this time of year. I guess there will always be transfer stories concerning us as we are a club that is always looking to strengthen where possible, though many of the reports that I have read are completely wide of the mark.'

With the media focusing on who could be set to leave White Hart Lane, Jol again showed his ambition to make Spurs into a force to be reckoned with both domestically and on the European front, when he beat London rivals West Ham to the signing of relegated Charlton's top scorer Darren Bent for a club record fee of £16.5 million. And the prolific striker who bagged 31 goals during his time at The Valley, revealed in his first interview with the club's website, his delight at joining a Spurs squad brimming with international talent: 'Tottenham have a lot of young English players and it's a young squad, it's a squad going forward and that's the direction I wanted to take. They seem to be getting better and better every season and I would love to be part of that. It helps a lot that I know a few of the lads from England internationals and I'm sure they will help me settle in. It's exciting times for me and the club, hopefully I'll show what I can do at Tottenham and we'll go on to win things.'

Despite already having Berbatov, Robbie Keane, Jermain Defoe and Mido on the payroll, Jol outlined his reasons for bringing in a fifth striker: 'Darren's strength is his stamina. Normally players will make runs three or four times in 45 minutes, he will do it all the time and if you manage to play balls behind the defence, he will be there. That's what I like about him. He has pace, he links play well and can see a pass – he can exploit the space and play as well. He knows Spurs is the place to be and that's something to be proud of.'

And Jol wasted no time in continuing his summer spending spree with the capture of France's Under-21 captain and centre back Younes Kaboul for £8 million from Auxerre, to strengthen the backline. With Spurs looking to improve on a second top five Premier League finish in successive seasons and break the dominance of the 'big four', Jol revealed in a summer interview with *World Soccer* the areas of the team that were still in need of improvement if they were to progress and finish the season in a Champions League place:

'We conceded more than 50 goals last season, which is too many to get into the top four. Also, we scored only 60 goals, again not enough to be in the top four. Dimitar Berbatov scored only 12 in the League, Robbie Keane 11, Jermain Defoe 10. That's not enough for a striker at a club wanting to be in the top four. So it's simple – we need to score more and concede fewer. In two years someone like Bale would be good enough for Manchester United, but he will be playing for Tottenham. The same goes for Aaron Lennon; who knows how good he could be? Guys like Berbatov, Keane and Darren Bent will still be top players by then, so at that point we will go for the Premier League title. If the players we have here progress as I expect, the sky is the limit.'

And when asked if it was vital that the club retained the services of top scorer Berbatov with a number of club's reported to be interested in the Bulgarian, Jol answered: 'It was never an issue. There was a lot of talk about Manchester United, but the chairman would never have sanctioned a move for a player who did so well for us last time. You can see why other clubs might like him, but he is very happy at Tottenham. Our slogan in the dressing room is the team is the star, not Berbatov, Keane or [Paul] Robinson. That is probably what someone like Berbatov likes about this club.'

The pre-season programme began with two away victories over Stevenage Borough and St. Patricks Athletic before the squad headed out to South Africa to face three matches in the Vodacom Challenge. Berbatov, who had missed Spurs' opening two friendlies, started the game against Kaiser Chiefs alongside regular strike partner Keane with new signing Bent starting the match on the bench. Keane opened the scoring for the Lilywhites early in the first half but the South African side netted to draw level five minutes after the break. Jol introduced Bent to the action just before the hour mark and the substitution paid immediate dividends when the striker sped down the left wing before squaring to the unmarked Berbatov for an easy tap in, his first of the season, which proved to be the winner.

Three days later Jol decided to rotate his squad as preparations for the new season continued, resting Berbatov and retaining only three players from the win over Kaiser Chiefs. The team recorded another victory, their fourth of pre-season, over Orlando Pirates, 2-1. However, Berbatov returned for the final match of the Vodacom Challenge partnering Bent up front, and the deadly duo provided the killer touch to ward off the challenge of Orlando once again with three goals in 21 first half minutes. Bent helped himself to another two goals to take his tally in pre-season to four and once again provided Berbatov with a simple finish to give Spurs their first trophy, albeit a minor one, under Jol's leadership.

Spurs defeated North London neighbours Leyton Orient 4-2 in a thrilling penultimate game of pre-season before returning to White Hart Lane for their final warm up against former Turin giants Torino ahead of the start of the league campaign. Before kick-off, new signings Gareth Bale, Darren Bent, Younes Kaboul and Kevin-Prince Boateng, who joined from Hertha Berlin just days before the match, were paraded to the home crowd, who collectively hoped the new blood could help them break into the top four and win a trophy for the first time in nine years.

Speaking to the club website on the eve of the Torino match, Boateng revealed that he hoped to emulate Berbatov's success in England following the Bulgarian's own move to Spurs from the Bundesliga at the beginning of the previous season. The 20-year-old German Under-21 midfielder, who won the award for Best Young Player in Germany in 2006, said:

'Of course I know Dimitar from the Bundesliga. He's a very good player and he could go to any league in the world and be the best there as well, he's that good. He scored against Hertha Berlin on a couple of occasions and the defensive players would always say to me "Kevin, how can we stop him?" and that's because he's such a great player. I went on the website and looked at the ages [of his new team-mates] – 19, 20, 21, 22 – and they are all big players. That's why I'm sure I can do big things for this team. I can learn a lot from this team and this league and I hope I'll become better and better. The spirit of this team is like a big family and that's what I need, I get the feeling everyone works together here.'

A 2-0 victory over the Italians, thanks to goals from Keane and Berbatov, ensured Spurs finished their pre-season campaign with a maximum seven victories from seven and also extended the team's record of 23 friendly matches unbeaten under Jol's stewardship, to ensure the team entered the new season in confident manner. And after notching his third goal of pre-season in the win over Torino, Berbatov mentioned his appreciation of the crowd's reaction to his name being announced before kick-off amid all the rumours of a potential transfer, and also his personal hopes for the forthcoming season ahead of the big kick-off against Sunderland: 'I really appreciate it, I am always a little uncomfortable with it, but I am really happy that they are happy with my performances and I will continue in this way. We're happy that the first game is almost here and I think we are prepared for it. We have one week left, we will get better and hopefully we can take three points from the game at Sunderland.'

And so, with a fantastic pre-season campaign behind them, the team set off for the North East in confident mood and in search of an early three points against Roy Keane's newly promoted Sunderland at the Stadium of Light. However, one player not making the trip with the rest of the squad, but who would be heading north permanently was Mido. The Egyptian striker agreed a transfer to Middlesbrough on the eve of the match with the Black Cats after seeing his chances of regular football further diminish with the arrival of Bent earlier in the summer.

Jol chose to start the match with Berbatov and Keane leading the attack, with Bent having to be content with a place on the substitutes' bench. The first half saw both sides create chances to break the deadlock in the season's curtain-raiser with Spurs goalkeeper Paul Robinson producing the best save of the first half from Daryl Murphy. Then, with only minutes of the first period remaining Berbatov burst forward into space breaking the Sunderland offside trap in the process before rounding goalkeeper Craig Gordon to put himself into a position to break the deadlock. However, centre-back Paul McShane managed to regain ground on the Bulgarian and put in a last-ditch tackle to prevent a certain goal. And despite Spurs' appeals for a penalty, the referee waved away the claims to leave the score goalless at the break.

With Spurs' front two struggling to penetrate the Sunderland defence, Jol introduced Bent to the action with 30 minutes remaining in place of Teemu Tainio, but despite one chance for Berbatov, which the striker scooped over the bar, Spurs were still unable to break through Sunderland's impregnable rearguard action. With just over 10 minutes left to play, Jol sent on Defoe in place of Berbatov as he sought to try and find a winning goal. But, with only seconds of the match remaining, Sunderland's new £5 million signing Michael Chopra found space in the Spurs area to calmly slot home a winner for the home side. Spurs had lost their opening match of the season for the second season in a row.

After the match, a clearly frustrated Jol revealed his unhappiness at the performance of his strikers during the match and their lack of workrate throughout: 'I can blame the strikers and I felt they didn't work hard enough or move enough. But on the other hand the midfield should have been more creative and they weren't.'

After being replaced by Bent in the second half of the defeat, Berbatov was visibly displeased with his manager's decision to substitute him. However, Jol refused to openly criticise his star striker for his actions, preferring instead to deliver his reasons for making the substitution: 'Berbatov is a very good player but I feel we needed a bit more urgency to score a goal against a team like Sunderland. We needed to get a sort of cushion and we didn't. We didn't see it coming but if you don't score with the quality we've got it is always possible the opposition will score a goal and they did.'

Three days later the team had an opportunity to make amends for their opening day defeat when they welcomed David Moyes' Everton team to White Hart Lane for the first home match of the season. After failing to seriously threaten the Sunderland defence the previous weekend, Jol shuffled his pack to include Berbatov – despite his reaction to being substituted – Keane and Bent in his starting line up, in the hope an added striker could make them more potent in front of goal.

But it was at the back that Spurs really struggled as Joleon Lescott managed to lose his marker Anthony Gardner to head home from Mikel Arteta's free-kick after just three minutes of the match. Bent was then denied his first league goal for the club when the linesman's flag called him back for offside, before Joseph Yobo threw himself in front of a shot from Berbatov to prevent an almost instantaneous equaliser.

Spurs' cause wasn't helped just before the 20-minute mark either when a suspected hamstring injury put an end to Younes Kaboul's home debut. However, in a reversal of fortunes from a Jermaine Jenas corner, Gardner this time managed to lose Everton goalscorer Lescott to head home a first half equaliser. But Spurs contrived to undo their good work 10 minutes later when Ricardo Rocha was only able to clear a cross from Arteta into the path of Leon Osman, who rammed the ball home for a 2-1 lead. And with first half stoppage time winding down, Everton further extended their lead when a free-kick from Alan Stubbs took a nasty deflection off Didier Zokora and flew past Robinson into the net.

There was enough time for Berbatov to be foiled by the woodwork from a Pascal Chimbonda cross before half-time, but the Bulgarian's night came to a disappointing early end when he pulled up injured as Jol's team failed to force their way back into the game and fell to their second defeat in a row. The following day, Jol revealed that both Berbatov and Kaboul would be missing for a few weeks, when he told the club website: 'We've had a couple more blows. Younes Kaboul will be out for the next three or four weeks with the hamstring injury he suffered against Everton, that's a real kick in the teeth and Dimitar Berbatov has a groin problem. It's an old problem and he will now visit a specialist in Germany. He will be out for a couple of weeks.'

After an examination of Berbatov's injury, there was some good news for Spurs when the prognosis suggested the talismanic forward would not be out for as long as had been first feared, but the Bulgarian's agent, Emil Dantchev revealed that his client would definitely miss the club's match against Derby County and would be a major doubt for the forthcoming Euro 2008 qualifier against Holland in Amsterdam. Dantchev said on Bulgarian radio station, *Darik*: 'I can't say when exactly he will be ready to play. He'll definitely miss the Derby County match but I hope he'll recover in time to play for the national team. He felt some pain in his adductor muscle in the last minute of the Everton match on Tuesday. The scan revealed that he sustained a niggling strain and he flew to Munich for consultations.'

Following two defeats from two matches which left Spurs – who had been expected to challenge strongly for a top four position – bottom in the early season Premier League table, Jol felt compelled to come out and deny the rumours that his position as head coach was under threat already. Speaking defiantly to *Sky Sports News,* Jol said:

'I can assure you that I saw the chairman last week and the week before, so there was no different situation. Of course, like me, he is worried, because of all the players who are out, and he hopes we can do better in the future. He assured me he was in the same boat because he is responsible as well. The only thing I have to do sometimes is take the pressure off him and tell him that things will be okay, and that is what I did yesterday. The players have to show more and they will. It has been a bad spell but the season is about a lot of chapters and we have not even had one chapter. We feel rotten about it and we will do something about it as we did over the last couple of seasons.'

With Berbatov ruled out through injury, the team eased the pressure on Jol when they easily beat newly-promoted Derby County 4-0 as two goals from Steed Malbranque and a fantastic individual goal from Jenas put the team 3-0 ahead with only 15 minutes played. Bent added a simple fourth, and his first competitive goal for the club, from close range with 20 minutes remaining to wrap up a comprehensive first victory of the season for Jol's much-criticised team.

Yet, despite the resounding victory over Derby, media speculation continued to suggest that Jol was living on borrowed time and that chairman Daniel Levy was lining up a move to bring Sevilla head coach, Juande Ramos to White Hart Lane to replace the popular Dutchman in the Spurs hotseat. However, Ramos denied the rumours held any truth when he spoke with Sevilla's official website ahead of the club's Spanish Super Club contest with Real Madrid. Ramos said: 'Curiously, when we play an important game like this news of this kind always comes out. I don't know what the motivation is. All our attention should be on the match and I totally deny that we had a meeting. I think this has been done to unsettle us. News like this comes out every day and we cannot reply to stories like this. I was in the hotel [that Spurs officials were at] because a friend came who had nothing to do with football.'

With only 10 days of the summer transfer window remaining and speculation rising as to who would move where in the last deals before the window's closure, ambitious Spurs, who had already spent a fortune in the summer, were sensationally linked with a move for Argentine superstar Juan Roman Riquelme. The Villarreal playmaker's agent Marcos Franchi admitted the North London club had submitted a bid to secure his client's signature. Franchi told *Radio La Red*:

'Despite that we haven't been told anything officially, we know that Villarreal has received a very important offer from Tottenham and that the president Fernando Roig is analysing it. They have to make a decision before 31 August, otherwise Riquelme will stay at Villarreal as there aren't any other serious negotiations. If nothing new appears I think that they should accept this offer as it is good for the club and the player. I don't think that Riquelme would be useful for Villarreal without playing. It would be much more useful for them to sell him so they recover what they invested in him when they bought him.'

But the excitement surrounding the potential move for the exciting Latin footballer from Buenos Aires evaporated almost as quickly as it had arisen when Villarreal announced that a deal had been reached for the permanent transfer of Riquelme back to his former club, Boca Juniors.

Meanwhile, following a midweek board meeting during which Jol's position and future, and that of his coaching staff, was put heavily under the microscope, Levy announced: 'We have had two good, progressive seasons with fifth place finishes. I am an ambitious chairman, we are an ambitious club and we want Champions League football at White Hart Lane. We, the board, owe it to the club and the supporters to constantly assess our position and performance and to ensure that we have the ability to operate and compete at that level. We have made a massive investment in the squad and as a result we have the best squad of players this club has had for over 20 years and they are equally hungry for success and silverware. For that we need our management and coaching standards to be of the highest quality such that players can fulfil their potential and we can compete with the best. We have discussed all of these expectations with Martin and he has confirmed to me today that he feels he is equipped with a squad and a determination to take on that challenge.'

And reacting to the news Jol admitted: 'We had a full and frank conversation and I fully understand the ambitions of the club – they are the same as those of the supporters. He has put a lot of hard work into this Club and with the squad of players we have assembled, it is realistic that we should look to challenge for a top four position and I have assured him and the Board that that is what I shall aim for. The last two seasons we have finished fifth and this season we start with an even better team. So we should be optimistic. Yes, it is pressure to deliver, but that is what we managers should expect. Hopefully all the media will relax now – all I shall be concentrating on is each and every game.'

With Jol's position apparently confirmed as secure for the time being, the media attention once again turned to the future of Berbatov, who was ready to return to the squad after a quick recovery from a groin injury. With only a week of the window remaining, Jol once again announced his determination to hold onto Berbatov, who had finished his first season in England as Spurs' top scorer:

'I told Dimitar that I love him and he told me that he loves me as well. He thanked me for bringing him over here and I said I would rather die than sell him. I also told one manager that [inquired about him] that I would rather die than sell Dimitar Berbatov. Berba knows that because I said the same to him. So for me there's no issue. Berbatov will stay at this club and he will play for us. The disappointing thing is that somebody maybe told one of the papers that I wanted to sell Dimitar.'

But despite Jol's claims that Berbatov would be going nowhere, the Bulgarian's agent, Emil Dantchev, revealed on Bulgarian radio station *Darik*, that he had been speaking with the Spurs hierarchy about alleged interest in his client from Manchester United. Dantchev said:

'We had a 90-minute meeting with Tottenham's chairman Daniel Levy and with sporting director Damien Comolli over Dimitar's future. They informed us that there's a query from Manchester United about the possibility of Berbatov joining them. They [Tottenham bosses] let us believe that they want Dimitar to stay for another season because they have ambitions to finish among the top four teams in the Premiership but they told us they'll have a meeting in the next day or two to decide his future.'

However, Manchester United chief executive David

Gill was quick to deny Dantchev's claims and the rumours linking the champions with a move for the classy Bulgarian when he told the Manchester United official website: 'Manchester United is linked with many players in every transfer window. The club has categorically not made a bid for Dimitar Berbatov.'

Although Gill was adamant that United had not launched a bid to try and secure Berbatov's signature, Sir Alex Ferguson, who signed West Ham's Argentine superstar Carlos Tevez in early August, did admit to Manchester radio station XFM that he had been interested in signing the player earlier in the summer, but that their overtures had been refuted by Spurs and were unlikely to change: 'We made an inquiry about a striker not so long ago. The club concerned would not sell and it remains that way. With a week to the transfer deadline, it would be impossible to get anyone else in now.'

With his future very much under the spotlight, the fit-again Berbatov returned to the Spurs starting lineup for the trip to face United at Old Trafford. And early in the first half, a neat flick from Berbatov set up Keane for a shot which touched the top of the crossbar as Spurs threatened Edwin van der Sar's goal. The scores remained level at half-time but Spurs twice threatened to take the lead in the second half when Berbatov nutmegged the champion's Dutch goalkeeper only to see his goalbound shot cleared off the line by Rio Ferdinand, before a last-ditch tackle from Wes Brown prevented Berbatov from opening the scoring, although Berbatov clearly felt the ball had struck the England international's hand and that Spurs should have been awarded a penalty. However, with penalties awarded at the Theatre of Dreams to the away team an almost non event, Spurs were denied the opportunity of a rare win at the home of the champions, and were further punished when Portuguese winger Nani hammered home a 30 yard winner to condemn Jol's team to a third defeat in four games.

The same day, Paul Kemsley, Spurs' vice-chairman issued an apology to the club's fans and head coach Martin Jol in the *News Of The World*, after it had been revealed that club officials had been seen meeting with Sevilla's Juande Ramos to discuss taking over from Jol if, as Kemsley suggested, the Dutchman should decide to depart the club. Kemsley said:

'I am sorry about last weekend's escapade and for the damage and upset it has caused to both Martin Jol, the club and the supporters. The truth is that we never offered Martin's job to Juande Ramos no matter what anybody thinks. I went to Seville for two reasons. Firstly to talk with Sevilla about the way they run their club and to discuss their model for success because that's what I want for Tottenham – success. You must believe I want what's best for the club and I think you should always talk to other people, especially successful people, to see how they have achieved so much. I must admit the second reason I was there was as a contingency against Martin leaving. I know Martin is hugely ambitious, he is always telling me that, and I know he is a coveted manager. There are a lot of teams out there who would love him in charge of their club. I think he is great but I'm worried he could leave. So you must have a contingency plan. I am not trying to force Martin out. I am 100 per cent behind him and I know Daniel Levy is 100 per cent behind him too. The events of the last week might not have given that impression and I regret that.'

With only days of the transfer window remaining and the futures of both Jol and Berbatov under the constant scrutiny of the world's media, the Bulgarian striker delivered a blow to any potential suitors and joy to the Spurs faithful when he distanced himself from a move away from North London in an interview with a Bulgarian football magazine.

'I chose to join Tottenham last season, now I'm staying at the club through my own free will, at least for now. No one said that United didn't have interest in me and my price in general but it has to be clear that there will not be a move for now. There has been a lot of speculation but all I can say now is that this saga has strengthened [Tottenham manager Martin] Jol's position and that the club's board decided to raise my salary.'

In the meantime, Spurs were awarded what appeared a favourable looking first round tie against Cypriot club Anorthosis Famagusta when the UEFA Cup first round draw took place at the end of August. The club received a somewhat more difficult proposition to progress from the third round of the Carling Cup however when they were given a home tie against fellow Premiership club, Middlesbrough. On the transfer front, there was good news for the Spurs fans when the club retained all of their top stars including Berbatov as the transfer window slammed shut until January, although the club did allow former Liverpool and Charlton midfielder, Danny Murphy to join Fulham on a permanent transfer.

Back in the league, Spurs missed a glorious opportunity to collect a second victory of the season when they contrived to throw away a 2-0 and 3-1 lead at Craven Cottage as they allowed Fulham to snatch a share of the spoils despite dominating the match from start to finish. Younes Kaboul opened the scoring with his first goal in a Spurs shirt when he latched onto a mistake from Fulham keeper Antti Niemi to poke the ball home. And the lead was doubled with just 25 minutes gone when Berbatov sprinted onto a through ball from Keane to unleash an unstoppable shot past the helpless Niemi. Fulham reduced the arrears before half-time through a Clint Dempsey header before Gareth Bale scored his own first goal for the club to extend the lead to two goals once again. Berbatov nearly added a fourth soon after only to see his effort cleared off the line by Chris Baird. However, Spurs' defensive woes were again exploited to the maximum as Fulham struck back to gain a point when Alexei Smertin and Diomansy Kamara on the stroke of full time levelled the score at 3-3.

After a break for crucial Euro 2008 qualifiers, which saw Berbatov and his Bulgarian compatriots fall to a 2-0 defeat at the hands of their Dutch hosts in Amsterdam before bouncing back with two goals from their irreplaceable captain to beat Luxembourg 3-0 in Sofia, Spurs' international stars returned to Spurs Lodge to prepare for the following weekend's first derby of the season at home to sworn enemies Arsenal. With Spurs determined to reclaim the North London bragging rights after a loss and a draw in both the league and the Carling Cup the previous season, Berbatov revealed that all the playing staff were firmly behind Martin Jol, despite the continuing rumours that the board were contemplating replacing him with Sevilla coach Juande Ramos, as the Dutchman sought to reignite Spurs season with a win against their bitter rivals. He told *The Sun*:

'The start to this season has been pretty much like the beginning of last season. That didn't go according to plan, but look how we ended up. We finished fifth and I am sure we can push on this time around. No one is worried. We have some great players and a real belief about us. Nothing will put us off. Everyone is behind the boss and we are ready to do even better. People ask us if everything is back to normal now, but it has been normal all the time. There has never been any problem from inside the camp. We support each other. With a derby to play, everyone is ready. Did it surprise me what people were saying about Martin? None of us want to talk about that any more. We are all behind him.'

Yet despite taking an early lead over the Gunners when Gareth Bale sent the majority of fans inside White Hart Lane wild with excitement after striking a superb free-kick – awarded for a foul on Berbatov – past the despairing dive of Arsenal goalkeeper Manuel Almunia to put Spurs in the driving seat with only 15 minutes played, Arsenal struck back three times to extend their unbeaten run against Spurs since 1999 further still. Berbatov wasted a golden opportunity to extend the lead when he beat Almunia only for Kolo Toure to clear the danger. Jol's team continued to create chance after chance to double their advantage, but with 65 minutes played, Emmanuel Adebayor rose high above the Spurs defence to silence the euphoric home supporters and nod in the equaliser. Again Spurs had been punished by their own set-piece frailties.

Berbatov then saw Arsenal left-back Gael Clichy clear his goalbound effort off his own line twice in succession from Jenas' dangerous corner, before Fabregas further dampened the home support's mood of optimism that the day would be theirs, when he rifled home an outstanding shot from fully 30 yards to put the visitors 2-1 ahead. And with the game, and time, slipping away from Spurs once again, Adebayor confirmed that it would be the red half of North London celebrating that night when he volleyed home past a stranded Robinson in memorable fashion to secure a 3-1 win.

After the disappointment of yet another derby day defeat under his reign, beleaguered head coach Jol attempted to raise the spirits of his troops ahead of the UEFA Cup first round clash with Anothosis Famagusta. Speaking ahead of the clash, Jol also admitted to the club's website that he was looking for Berbatov to get back in and among the goals as soon as possible, after a slow start to the season which had thus far only seen him net once in five first team appearances.

'After the last season, you could say he is a slow starter', Jol said. 'After scoring he is always different. You need a bit of success, as a player and as a team. He is a quiet lad, but has confidence and shows it every day.'

Berbatov sat out an impressive 6-1 victory over the Cypriot team at the Lane, as goals from Kaboul, Michael Dawson, Keane, Bent and two from substitute Defoe secured only a second victory of the season for Jol's under-achieving team. After the win, Jol admitted his delight at witnessing three of his four strikers hitting the back of the net, and admitted that he welcomed the headache that they were providing him with to the BBC: 'Robbie Keane could have scored three, Darren Bent took his goal and Dimitar Berbatov was our top scorer in Europe last season. If they push me all the time it makes it difficult for me.'

Despite Spurs' poor start to the season and being left on the bench for the duration of the midweek UEFA Cup win, Berbatov revealed in an interview with the *Sunday Mirror* his happiness at playing for the club under the leadership of Jol, insisting that he was happy to still be at the club despite rumoured interest in the summer:

'I'm a big fan. He is one of the reasons I came here. The players respect him and they enjoy working for him. I respect him and I will stand by him. I have played under a lot of coaches but he is one of the best. I don't care for speculation. People talk about me because of what I did last season and that's normal. Am I happy here? What do you think? Loyalty is important to me and there is a debt to be repaid. Spurs wanted me no matter what – where were these other clubs then? If I leave it's because I'm no longer wanted. I won't ask for a move – I'm very settled and happy.'

And the Bulgarian captain also revealed his reasons for deciding to move to England despite his own reservations that the league wouldn't suit his style of play: 'I used to watch English football in Germany and thought I will never be able to make it there. It was too fast, too physical and I just thought "this could be embarrassing".

But I knew I had to come. If hadn't made the move I would have regretted it for the rest of my life.'

And fellow striker Darren Bent reiterated Berbatov's support for Jol, saying: 'The pressure on him is unfair. He finished fifth two seasons in a row so it's unjustified. We don't know what goes on upstairs but the players all love the gaffer and the fans do too. We want to show that on the pitch.'

Spurs travelled north to face struggling Sammy Lee's Bolton Wanderers in their next match as Jol's team continued to search for only a second league win of the season against their perennial bogey team. Spurs threatened to take the lead with 25 minutes played when Jussi Jaaskelainen produced a great save to deny Berbatov from a tight angle, but Spurs only had to wait a further eight minutes before Keane broke the deadlock from close range with his first league strike of the new campaign. Just five minutes later however, Ivan Campo, who was making his first start of the season, pounced to head home a free-kick from El-Hadji Diouf to square the scores. Teemu Tainio, Steed Malbranque and Keane came close to grabbing a winner for the away team but Bolton held out to deny Spurs a much-needed win.

The team bounced back the following Wednesday to knock Gareth Southgate's Middlesbrough out of the Carling Cup and give Jol some respite from the team's lacklustre league form. After a goalless first period, second half goals from Bale and Tom Huddlestone ensured Spurs would be in the draw for the fourth round of the cup.

With the team still struggling to find their form of the

last two seasons as October approached, Spurs chairman Daniel Levy admitted on Setanta Sports *Friday Football Show* that there had been an element of truth to the rumours earlier in the month that they were lining up a replacement for Jol:

'Obviously with any speculation sometimes there's an element of truth, but there has been a lot of stuff that's been written in the papers which has just been completely untrue. I think it's inevitable with the quality of players we have in this squad that when we're not performing on the pitch there's bound to be speculation. I've made it very clear that I very much want Martin to succeed, Martin is fully aware of our ambition, he also has got ambition – he just needs to get the results. I think we're all fairly thick-skinned if I'm honest, I just think Martin and the players need to ignore the outside pressure and just win, and that's what it's all about.'

Meanwhile, with Spurs' defence struggling to keep clean sheets, Jol revealed that captain and defensive rock Ledley King was still some way from full fitness following surgery on his long-standing knee injury: 'He is progressing. I cannot push him. He is not doing everything [in training]. He is not doing the overloading, the one-v-ones, the sprints. He is doing the normal work.'

Ahead of Spurs' 125th anniversary match with Aston Villa at the Lane, Berbatov admitted to *Sky Sports News* that he was unhappy with his early season form following an outstanding first campaign at the club, and that he and his fellow team-mates were putting extra hours in at the training ground in an attempt to improve the club's fortunes. Commenting on the 'second season is more difficult' suggestion, Berbatov commented:

'Maybe that's it. But it doesn't mean that I should not score, and that's why I work hard to improve myself, because last year was really good for me, and nobody knew me. But now maybe everyone knows how I play it's more difficult for me, but that's not an excuse for me and I will keep working harder and harder to push myself and the team. Sometimes you play well and you lose games, but in football the only thing that matters is the result. And we will try to do that, to win points. Not only me, just everyone who wants to develop stays after training to do a shootout and some exercises. The thing is the gaffer and [assistant boss] Chris Hughton are always trying to teach us.'

Ahead of the match with Villa, Spurs received a welcome boost. Their hopes of progressing in the Carling Cup were significantly boosted when they avoided potential Premier League opposition in the draw and were paired with Championship outfit Blackpool.

Spurs went into the match with Villa looking to kick-start their season with a morale-boosting win on the anniversary of the club's formation in front of a plethora of the club's legendary former stars. And, although Berbatov finally grabbed only his second goal of the season with a powerful header from Huddlestone's corner, Spurs' leaky defence capitulated yet again as Villa raced into a 4-1 lead following some shocking defending and goals from Martin Laursen, who helped himself to a brace and further goals for Craig Gardner and Gabriel Agbonlahor.

Pascal Chimbonda responded quickest to a shot from Jermain Defoe which rebounded to him off a post to pull a goal back for Spurs with the clock winding down, before Keane fired home a penalty to bring Spurs within a goal of the visitors. And with only seconds of the match remaining Kaboul hammered home after Villa failed to deal with a corner to cap a fantastic fightback and send the fans wild on a special night for everyone associated with the club.

A 1-1 draw in Cyprus with Famagusta in midweek, courtesy of a penalty from Keane ensured Spurs progressed 7-2 on aggregate to the draw for the group stage of the UEFA Cup. Next up in the league was a tough game against Liverpool at Anfield.

The match represented a clash of the under-pressure managers with Jol struggling to get his team going and Rafa Benitez seeing his side struggling in the league and also looking likely to crash out of the Champions League at the group stage. Liverpool's summer signing Andriy Voronin, who had played alongside Berbatov at Leverkusen for two seasons before the Bulgarian departed for Spurs in 2006, opened the scoring early in the first half for the home side. He capitalised on a mistake from Robinson in the Spurs goal to prod home from close-range after the England goalkeeper spilled a free-kick from Liverpool captain Steven Gerrard.

However, Keane equalised on the stroke of half-time when he latched on to a flick from Berbatov after a long kick upfield from Robinson to poke home past Jose Reina and send the two sides in level at the break. And within seconds of the restart, Keane sent the travelling support into a frenzy of celebration, when he grabbed his second goal of the game with a carbon copy of his first. Robinson's long free-kick was once again flicked on by the impressive Berbatov into the path of Keane who remained calm to tuck the ball over the advancing Reina for the second time in the match.

With time running out for Liverpool to find an equaliser and prevent a first league defeat of the season, record-signing Fernando Torres climbed highest to head home a cross from full back Steve Finnan and secure a fortunate point, and in the process deny Spurs only their second win of the Premier League season.

Two days after the disappointing 2-2 draw with Liverpool, Spurs were handed a relatively good draw for the group stage of the UEFA Cup when they were paired with Anderlecht, Getafe, Hapoel Tel Aviv and Aalborg.

Despite insisting that the group wouldn't be easy to qualify from, Jol told the club website that he was confident that his team could finish in the top three to qualify for the next stage of the competition, after reaching the quarter-final stage the previous season. He said: 'I am pretty satisfied. You can only assess it on paper at the moment and my feeling is that it could have been a lot tougher for us. Anderlecht away will be a hard one, but it is the final game for us and hopefully we will have done the business by then. They have got fanatical supporters, just like we've got, so that should be a special night with the history between the two clubs in this competition. It is good that we start at home against Getafe before we face a trip to Tel Aviv. People tend to under-estimate the football in Israel, but they have got players there from all over the world so that could well be a tricky game and there is always a great atmosphere. Aalborg will not be easy, they came through a tie against Sampdoria and I am pleased we have got them at home. Everybody enjoyed themselves last season, we wanted the European nights back and we had some great games at home and away at the likes of Besiktas and Leverkusen. We are looking forward to more of the same.'

Domestic action once again took a two week break to accommodate the Euro 2008 qualifiers after the Liverpool match and for Berbatov and his Bulgarian team mates, it was imperative that they defeated Albania in Tirana to keep alive their hopes of pipping the Dutch to qualification. An unfortunate first half own goal from Radostin Kishishev left the team facing an uphill struggle but not for first time in his international career, the ever-reliable Berbatov provided a clinical finish to bring the scores level with just three minutes remaining and offer Bulgaria hope.

However, hope quickly turned to desperation in injury time when a defender Igor Tomasic was penalised for a handball and the referee awarded Albania a spot-kick, only for goalkeeper Georgi Petkov to save superbly and maintain Bulgaria's slight chance of qualifying for the finals. However, their fate now rested in the hands of Luxembourg who would need to take at least a point off the Dutch in the next set of qualifiers to give Bulgaria any chance of a place in Austria and Switzerland.

Back in England and on the eve of the Premier League match with Newcastle, Berbatov received a major boost in confidence when he was named on the

preliminary shortlist of 50 players for the prestigious
Ballon d'Or award, in recognition of his first season in
England with Spurs

On the eve of the match with Newcastle, Berbatov
received a major boost in confidence when he was named
on the preliminary shortlist of 50 players for the
prestigious Ballon d'Or award, in recognition of his first
season in England with Spurs. His inclusion ensured he
was the first Spurs player since David Ginola in 1999 to
make the shortlist for the accolade voted for by
journalists from every member country of UEFA.

With Spurs still struggling down in the lower echelons
of the Premier League table, the team looked ahead to the
away clash at Newcastle as an opportunity to relieve the
pressure on Jol and the rest of the coaching staff.
Berbatov began the match at St. James' Park on the
bench as Jol opted to start with Keane and Bent as his
forward partnership. With the scores level at 0-0 as the
half-time interval approached, it was Newcastle who
broke the stalemate when Nigerian striker Obafemi
Martins lashed home an unstoppable shot from an acute
angle past Radek Cerny in the Spurs goal to give the
Geordies the lead going into the break.

And within five minutes of the restart, Spurs proceeded
to gift their hosts a vital second goal when defender
Claudio Cacapa was left completely unmarked at the
near post to head home Emre's cross. Keane reduced the
lead with a close-range finish after Bent's header
rebounded to him off a post, and Jol responded to the
goal by sending on Berbatov to boost his team's search
for an equaliser.

Unfortunately for Jol, however, James Milner then struck home a left-footed shot to seal the victory for Sam Allardyce's team and condemn Spurs to a fifth league defeat in only 10 matches to leave Jol on the brink of losing his position as head coach. After the match, Jol responded to allegations that Berbatov had undermined him and ignored his instructions to warm up three times from the substitutes' bench, with apparent surprise in an after-match interview with *The Guardian*:

'I've heard about this and it is rubbish – there was no problem. Dimitar knows exactly what the schedule is for him and he is fine. I don't know who this rubbish is coming from. He played when [Darren] Bent did not play for two weeks and he could train. I need him on Thursday [for the UEFA Cup clash with Getafe]. He knows that and I don't know where this rubbish is coming from.'

Nevertheless, the under-pressure Dutchman did admit that the hectic schedule of matches facing his team was proving to be something of a hindrance in their pursuit to climb the league table, but denied that the team were facing a crisis of confidence: 'You could say that was from the start of the season, but I cannot agree with that because if you lack confidence, you cannot lead 2-1 against Liverpool, come back from 4-1 down to 4-4 [against Aston Villa], be 3-1 up against Fulham and could have scored five. I feel if we get one result, the confidence will be there. But after the Liverpool game, they all went away on international duty and then we had to come to Newcastle, so the schedule doesn't help.'

But despite Jol's insistence that Berbatov hadn't refused

to warm up when instructed to do so, Portsmouth manager Harry Redknapp wrote in his column in *The Sun* that Jol would perhaps be better off without the Bulgarian allegedly disrupting the harmony in the Spurs camp. He wrote:

'The very last thing Martin Jol needs right now is Dimitar Berbatov spitting his dummy out because he's not in Tottenham's starting team every week. You only find out the true character of your players when the chips are down and the pressure is on. And we all saw what Berbatov is made of when he was sat sulking on the bench at Newcastle the other night with a face like a big baby. Everyone knows what a terrific player the Bulgarian can be. But he's not the striker he was a year ago and, from what I've seen, he looks to be disinterested and playing for himself rather than his team. His attitude is terrible and his behaviour at St James' Park sent out all the wrong signals.

'Maybe he's sulking because he didn't get a move to Manchester United in the summer. But he's done himself absolutely no favours on that account because I know for a fact Alex Ferguson would never stand for any player who behaves the way Berbatov has done this week. When your team is in trouble you need the big characters to stand up. That's just what Robbie Keane has done for Spurs and Berbatov should show the same attitude. I have always believed that when you lose a player's support you get him out as quickly as possible. No matter how good, you're better off without him.'

However, despite Redknapp's comments, Jol decided to restore Berbatov to the starting lineup for the UEFA Cup match with Spanish side Getafe at the Lane. Before the match, the team gathered in a pre-match huddle as they attempted to show that the team spirit had not diminished despite the awful start to the season. However, with rumours around the stands suggesting that Jol's time as Spurs coach was set to be brought to an end after the match, the Spurs faithful, who had been unwavering in their support of their Dutch coach in recent weeks made their warm feelings for him known as they sang his name throughout the match.

But although Jermain Defoe put Spurs into an early lead, after Berbatov set him up with a header back across goal, Spurs defensive woes continued to be highlighted when they conceded the equaliser from yet another free-kick. Berbatov put the ball into the net to restore the lead only to see the linesman's flag up for an offside against strike partner Defoe. The Bulgarian forward later missed a wonderful opportunity to put Spurs ahead again when he somehow managed to head the ball wide when a goal seemed certain. And he was punished to the full when, with 20 minutes remaining, Getafe's Braulio struck to give the Spanish team the lead. Spurs squandered several chances to equalise late on and when Dawson saw his header crash against the bar, it became obvious that Jol's reign was destined to come to an end with a disappointing defeat.

In the aftermath of the defeat, Spurs chairman Daniel Levy moved to clear up the confusion surrounding the circumstances of Jol's departure from the White Hart Lane hotseat when he released a statement on the club's official statement stating that the board had reached agreement before the UEFA Cup match with Getafe to remove Jol from his position:

'We can confirm that the board has this evening asked Martin Jol, Club Manager and Chris Hughton, First Team Coach to stand down from their positions with immediate effect. We have not taken these decisions lightly or without recognition of the contribution both Martin and Chris have made to the club. For me, Martin and Chris' departure is regrettable. Our greatest wish was to see results turn in our favour and for there to be no need for change. We feel honoured that Martin has been manager at our club, having seen us qualify twice for Europe. Chris has been with us since 1977, bar a three-year period, both as player and coach and he has been an excellent ambassador for the club. They have been professional, popular and respected members of the coaching staff and there will always be a warm welcome for them both at the Lane.'

Following the club's decision to remove him and Hughton from their positions, Jol told the website: 'I can understand the position of the Club in light of the results. I have thoroughly enjoyed my time here. Tottenham Hotspur is a special club and I want to thank the terrific staff and players. For me the fans were always amazing with their support so I would also like to say thank you – I shall never forget them.'

CHAPTER 10

THE RAMOS REVOLUTION

*'I want to let everyone know that I am a Tottenham Hotspur player,
I love the club and everyone at the club.'*
DIMITAR BERBATOV

ollowing the departure of Jol and the subsequent resignation of Juan de la Cruz Ramos Cano from his position as Sevilla coach the day after Spurs' defeat at the hands of Getafe, the North London club issued a statement on the official club website confirming the Spaniard as the new club's new head coach: 'The Club is delighted to announce the appointment of Juande Ramos as Head Coach. The contract period runs until the end of the 2010–11 season.'

During his time as manager at Sevilla, Ramos, 53, had presided over the most successful period in the club's history having guided them to successive UEFA Cup triumphs in 2006 and 2007, a European Super Cup, a Copa del Rey and a Spanish Super Cup. Then he took the team to within one win of a first ever La Liga title, although they did secure Champions League qualification for the first time after finishing the campaign in third. Speaking to the Spurs website for the first time after being confirmed as the club's new manager, Ramos revealed his excitement at being given the chance to take over the reigns of one of England's biggest and most famous clubs:

'I greatly appreciate the opportunity to work as head coach at Tottenham Hotspur, a club with a great tradition and history. Ever since I started my coaching career I have wanted to work in England. It is my sincere hope that I can repay the faith the Spurs board has shown in me. I am looking forward to meeting the players. It is a squad any coach would be excited to work with. I genuinely believe that there is the potential to achieve great things together. I was hugely impressed with the Spurs fans both home and away when Sevilla played Spurs last season and it will be a privilege to be the coach of this club with the huge support it enjoys both at White Hart Lane and throughout the world.'

And sporting director Damien Comolli revealed the board's delight at the appointment, stressing that an improvement in results was now the priority under the new coaching team of Ramos, Marcos Alvarez – his former assistant at Sevilla – and former Spurs midfielder Gustavo Poyet, who left his position as Leeds United's Assistant Manager.

'Juande's arrival is great news for Tottenham Hotspur', said Comolli. 'He brings with him a wealth of experience, a proven track record and a winning pedigree. Now is the time for us to regroup and look to deliver the results and performances that everyone associated with the Club wants to see. By making the appointment at this stage of the season, with our current, talented group of players, we have given ourselves the opportunity to compete well in all four competitions. Juande is a highly respected coach and his agreement to join us is excellent news. I know he is eager to get started.'

Ramos had spoken in an exclusive interview with *World Soccer* in February 2007 about his thoughts on the possibility of managing in England one day, and also revealed that his agents had alerted him to the possibility of interest in his services from Spurs. He said: 'I'm a professional who's open to any job offer from anywhere in the world. I don't have any problem coaching anywhere. I heard about it through my agents but there was no direct contact. I really like the Premiership. English football is very attractive, and I certainly wouldn't rule it out. Football in England is fast, direct, attacking, aggressive – I like that. Also, Rafa Benitez has shown that Spaniards can coach there. There are some similarities between me and him – in fact, we have almost had parallel careers.'

The interview also revealed Ramos' philosophy on football, which he described as making his players believe they can achieve more all the time: 'The key is convincing the players to be very ambitious. Sometimes you can lose games, but you have to keep going with it, keep striving to achieve more. We've had a few bad results and come back from them. I try to make the players see that you can win or lose, but that there's a path you have to stick to. You can lose the match, but you can't lose your identity.'

And in the interview he also alleviated any fears that the fans may have had over his relationship with sporting directors in general with Martin Jol rumoured to have been irritated by Comolli in his position as sporting director during his time as head coach at Spurs. Ramos said: 'The thing is the coach doesn't really have time to do both jobs. What you need is trust and professionalism.'

Ramos took his seat in the directors' box for the team's next fixture against Mark Hughes' Blackburn Rovers at White Hart Lane, leaving Clive Allen and Alex Inglethorpe in charge of first team affairs for the day. Robbie Keane opened the scoring from the penalty spot five minutes after half-time when Stephen Warnock felled Aaron Lennon in the area to put Spurs in charge. Lennon nearly doubled the advantage before Blackburn's South African striker Benni McCarthy struck a deflected shot past Radek Cerny to level the scores with an hour played. Berbatov almost regained the lead for the home side only to see his goalbound header brilliantly saved by Rovers' American keeper Brad Friedel. And despite having the better of game overall, Spurs were punished with a sucker-punch in injury time when Christopher Samba curled home a delightful winning goal for Rovers to ensure the points would be returning north to Lancashire. The result also ensured that Spurs remained firmly entrenched in the relegation zone.

Ramos took charge of his new team for the first time on Halloween Night when Spurs faced Blackpool in the Carling Cup at the Lane. However, there were to be no tricks played on the Spaniard or his team by the Championship side as Keane turned home a flick from

Berbatov to give Spurs the lead before Pascal Chimbonda confirmed the team's place in the next round of the cup with a powerful header. Ramos' reward for steering Spurs into the fourth round of the cup was a quarter-final clash against former England coach, Sven-Goran Eriksson's Manchester City side at The City of Manchester stadium.

Following the victory over Blackpool, and with his first league match at Middlesbrough fast approaching, Ramos announced his intention to retain the services of Berbatov despite continuing rumours that the Bulgarian star was unhappy at the club: 'Obviously he's one of the best quality players we have got at the club and we want to have him with us for a long time to come. I'm sure he will have an excellent season. I've spoken to all the players collectively and in private, but I have not spoken to any of them about such a situation. I've seen him and he looks quite happy and very well integrated into the team, but I've only been here for a few days. I don't know if the way he is, whether this is his usual character, if he is happy or not. I don't know. I can't make that evaluation after only being here for a few days.'

And Ramos also took time out from preparations for the game at the Riverside to also praise Berbatov's strike partner Robbie Keane, adding: 'He's a great professional – I'm not going to discover that now. I know about the goals he has scored for the team, he is one of the captains of the team and he has this great experience which is very necessary for the young players coming through the team. They see him as a reference and it's very important that he passes on that experience.'

Nevertheless, Ramos displayed his intention to have little regard for player reputations when he chose to leave out both Berbatov and Keane from his starting line up to face Boro, preferring instead to partner Darren Bent with Jermain Defoe up front. And Bent repaid the faith shown in him by the new man at the helm to fire Spurs into a first half lead. However, Spurs once again displayed defensive ineptitude to let their lead slip when Luke Young snapped up a poor clearance to fire home a glorious shot from 25 yards to give Gareth Southgate's men a share of the points, leaving both teams languishing perilously close to the relegation places.

With two months remaining until the re-opening of the transfer window in January, sporting director Damien Comolli met with Berbatov's agent Emil Dantchev in early November to discuss the striker's future. And following the meeting Comolli revealed to the club website that despite Berbatov's struggle to reproduce his scintillating form of the previous season, Dantchev had assured him that the fans' idol was not looking to win himself a move away from White Hart Lane in January. Comolli said: 'It is simply not an issue. I met with Dimitar's agent and he assured me Dimitar is not looking for a move in January and simply wants to concentrate on helping the team push up the table. He is on a long-term contract with us and Juande sees him as an important part of our plans.'

Meanwhile, former supremo Martin Jol spoke out in an interview with the *Daily Express* and stated that he believed Berbatov and the rest of the squad had been aware before the UEFA Cup match with Getafe that the match would prove to be his last in charge of the club. Jol said: 'Something very strange happened just one minute before kick-off. Berbatov came over to me and said "Sorry boss! Come on!" I thought that perhaps he was regretting what had happened in the previous match at Newcastle, or that he hadn't given me his best before, but it didn't cross my mind that he and the rest of the players had already been told by friends who had been texting them that I had been sacked.'

And with Spurs still embroiled in a scrap to climb away from the relegation zone, Jol admitted that although he continued to admire Berbatov's ability as a player, the striker was not the best player to have in the side when the going gets tough. He said: 'At St James' Park, a lot had been made in the media about Berbatov's attitude, that he didn't want to come on because he was sulking at being on the bench. Normally Chris Hughton would tell the players to warm up, but not this time. However, he didn't seem that keen to do it. I turned my shoulder again and this time looked him in the eye and told him "come on, warm up" and he began to warm up. He never said he didn't want to come on, but that's how it has been perceived. But that's Berbatov. He always seems reluctant to do anything. Gifted? Yes. But he is not a fighter. Perhaps you need others who are fighters to balance out the team.'

Ramos vowed to *The Sun* that he was determined to get to the bottom of Berbatov's frustrating slump in form, saying: 'Berbatov is a great footballer. The reasons why he is not achieving his top form must be found.'

But the new incumbent of the Spurs hotseat also

revealed that he would never attempt to force an unhappy player to stay at a club if they had already set their mind on leaving: 'I believe you can't force players to stay in the team if they don't want to. It is not good for the team or the player, so I wouldn't stand in anyone's way if they want to leave. I think he is happy, but that is a question you need to ask him. He is a Spurs player and he needs to help and support the team.'

Ramos' assistant, Gus Poyet, admitted meanwhile that Spurs would not be looking to offload their prize asset with the transfer window creeping ever closer, telling *Sky Sports News*: 'Everybody starts talking because we are getting close to the transfer window, but from our point of view Berba is here, the same as the other three strikers, so we have to count on them. One day in football you are sure that something is not going on, and then the next morning you wake up and it is a news story in the papers, so we have to be ready for everything.'

And with a must-win game away at Hapoel Tel Aviv lying in wait for Spurs, Poyet revealed that Ramos had already pinpointed the UEFA Cup as a trophy his new charges were capable of winning: 'It is a big option to win a trophy. We were unlucky to lose the first game and we need to put it right straight away. It is one of the competitions that, with the quality in the team, we feel we can go all the way. He [Ramos] can make history by winning it three times, so it is important for us.'

On morning of the match with Hapoel, *The Sun* published an interview with Asen Berbatov, the younger brother of Dimitar, who they alleged told them of his brother's intention to move to a bigger team: 'In my opinion, Tottenham are OK. In Manchester, though, things will be better – much better. If United really want him, maybe he should go. I think it is his time to go. There is nothing more to do at Spurs. Dimitar is under-performing. He is feeling very good physically. But as regards everything else, it is a big disappointment – especially with the team dropping in the league. He doesn't feel very good emotionally. This is the reason that the games are not going well. My brother is like this. When the team has bad form, he goes into standby mode.'

Asen continued: 'He shares his secrets about everything, yet still we don't talk about the new coach. Sometimes he finds it better to withdraw from things and collect his thoughts. Nothing is changed. Everyone is looking for a way to escape from this situation. My brother is at this moment feeling depressed. The problem is he doesn't score and the team goes bad. The rumours about him do not bother him.

'I think he will stay in England. He likes the style of football. He has outgrown Spurs. He needs to find a bigger club. I think this next season he will go to a bigger club. Next season he will be in a club playing in the Champions League. His skill comes from his mental approach. When my brother is grumpy, his form is bad. I do not know why he is grumpy to everybody. I know him very well and I can see when he is playing now he is grumpy. On the pitch I can see he has lost the desire to perform. When team-mates close him from the game and don't pass to him, he switches off. I saw the Newcastle game and Spurs were abysmal. Even considering that my brother loves Newcastle but plays for Tottenham, when he is not the centre of attention and main man, he is grumpy.'

However, striking back at the constant conjecture regarding his own future amid fresh reports that one newspaper had quoted his father, Ivan, of revealing his son had told him he wanted a move away from North London, Berbatov issued a statement on the club website insisting his intention to remain at the club and work under Ramos.

He said: 'I don't like to speak too much and don't like to be in the spotlight or the papers. I just want to play football. There has been a lot of stuff written about me leaving. I haven't said anything until now, but they are now involving my family and I cannot allow that. When somebody is writing lies about my family I must get involved. I am my own man, when I want to speak I will and I will tell you the truth no matter how hard it is. That is why I am talking now. I want to let everyone know that I am a Tottenham Hotspur player and I love the club and everyone at the club. I don't always smile so much, but that does not make me a bad person. I don't smile because we are near the bottom of the table and have not been playing well – I have not been playing well either. The worst thing is when someone starts writing lies and when people see that they start to believe it. That really is the worst thing.

'I just want to say that I am here, I am happy here and I will help the club in any way I can. The fans love the club and they have been behind me ever since my first game. I appreciate them the most and I want to tell them that I am not going anywhere. I have a contract and I will give my best, for now it is not going so well for me because all the writing in the papers has been messing with my head and I lost my concentration. I don't want to see my name in the papers anymore – I just want to play football and enjoy myself. When I see things in the paper with somebody telling lies about my father, how can I be calm? I am disappointed and I don't understand how somebody can write something like that – it is a lie. Bringing my family into it is the biggest sin.'

Spurs returned home from Israel with a 2-0 victory to reignite their hopes of progression in the UEFA Cup with Keane and Berbatov – both restored to the attack – grabbing the headlines with a goal apiece. But despite a satisfactory win, Ramos refused to pick out any individuals for special praise, telling the club's website:

'I believe in looking at a team rather than at any particular individual players. It's positive from the point of view that the players want to take advantage of all the opportunities. There were occasions when we should have done better to try to get another goal. That is possibly the reason why there were some differences between the players. But that ambition to do things well is positive. We didn't play well enough but after the two goals I felt better and I could think about Sunday. It was a typical UEFA Cup game and winning was very important for us after losing the first game. I was impressed with the performance, although we did not play at our best, and I was also thinking about the Wigan match. I saw the team grow in confidence and I am confident about Sunday's match.'

Ramos retained the Bulgarian in his starting XI for the home clash with Wigan three days after the Hapoel match and Berbatov produced one of his best performances of the season to help Spurs record only their second league victory of the season with a 4-0 demolition of managerless Wigan. Spurs raced into a 3-0 lead before half-time with midfielder Jermaine Jenas finding the net twice, racing onto Berbatov's defence-splitting pass to score the first. Later, the Bulgarian concocted a fantastic piece of skill to set up a third for Aaron Lennon to effectively finish the game with more than 45 minutes still remaining. And the Bulgarian, playing with a smile on his face, played a key role in setting up Spurs' fourth of the day when he showed great vision to find Lennon once again with a lovely ball, who this time passed the responsibility onto substitute Darren Bent to compound Wigan's misery.

And after inspiring the team to an easy victory, Poyet led the plaudits for Berbatov's performance when he told *Sky Sports*: 'Everybody was looking to see Berba. He knows that he is going to be in the papers and the television for the next two months until the window is open. But we need to make sure that he is happy here and that he keeps playing like he did today. There have been too many rumours. Of course you get frustrated. I think at the moment we need to calm down and wait. That is everyone. Wait and take your time. It is only November.'

A delighted Poyet also gave his verdict on the team's first three points under Ramos' new regime, claiming that the defence had been much more effective than previousl. 'It was definitely better', he said. 'It was important to keep a clean sheet and build at the back because it gave the rest of the team the freedom to go forward and show their qualities. That is the quality we know we have got, but we need to look at the whole team. We are doing well offensively, but also in defence. We have done nothing yet. We have to keep calm, but it was important to get the result here today.'

The day after the first league victory of his Spurs reign, Ramos admitted to *The Sun* that he was anxious for Berbatov to make a decision on his future one way or the other, so that he could make plans for the future: 'Dimi has already said he wants to continue in the team. I hope he's happy and he enjoys playing in the team and that we continue to get good results. I hope he will make a decision soon and I hope he will stay. His performance was good, in line with that of the team. I think he was magnificent and the team was thankful for it. When Berbatov is involved everything becomes more simple and, despite not scoring, he created a lot of chances.'

Meanwhile with Berbatov back home in Bulgaria to prepare for Bulgaria's crucial Euro 2008 qualifier against Romania, he told the Bulgarian website, gong.bg, of his initial impressions of Ramos: 'My first impression of him is that he's an incredible person. As a character, he talks to everybody on the team personally. He is a man who tries hard and he wants to help the team very much. He's the perfect one for the job.'

After coming out and declaring his happiness at working under Ramos' leadership, it looked as if the chances of him leaving in the January transfer window had receded greatly, yet former Spur Michael Carrick told the *Metro* newspaper that he would be delighted if the Bulgarian was to follow his lead in the future and quit White Hart Lane for Old Trafford. Carrick said: 'Any world-class player who is going to bring something different to the club, you always welcome that whether that's Berbatov or whoever. He's a very good player. I've watched him quite a bit because he's playing for my old club and I try and watch them whenever I can. He had a very good season last year and people are always going to link him with big clubs like United. As players here what you look for is a player coming in who can bring you something different, like Berbatov certainly would. I'm not saying he's better than what we've got, because we've got the best around up front. But we would welcome any world-class players who can strengthen the squad and Berbatov certainly would do that.'

Bulgaria's hopes of qualifying for the European Championship finals in Austria and Switzerland remained just about intact when they defeated Romania 1-0 in Sofia. However, confirmation that Holland had defeated Luxembourg 1-0 meant that Berbatov and his fellow countrymen's hopes of qualifying for a major tournament would now move onto the World Cup qualifiers for the 2010 World Cup in South Africa. Four days later Berbatov scored his sixth goal in 11 qualifiers to help Bulgaria to a 2-0 win in Slovenia to ensure they would finish in third place in their qualifying group.

On his return to action in England, Berbatov started the local derby against West Ham at Upton Park alongside Keane, and with just seven minutes played Berbatov appeared to be fouled in the area, only to see the referee wave away his appeals for a penalty. Things got worse for Spurs when West Ham gained the advantage in the 20th minute when Kaboul's attempted clearance struck Luis Boa Morte who cleverly set up Carlton Cole for the game's opening goal. Paul Robinson prevented West Ham from increasing their lead with a stunning point blank save from Boa Morte, before Berbatov somehow contrived to miss the target from six yards as he connected with a cross from Bale.

Spurs missed out on yet another stonewall penalty when the referee waved play on after West Ham keeper Robert Green felled Keane in the area, and the away side had to wait until the 66th minute for an equaliser when Dawson headed in from Jenas' free-kick. After coming on as a late replacement for Keane, Defoe had the opportunity to notch the winning goal against his former club when Lucas Neill brought him down in the area for a penalty that the referee this time awarded. But Green proved to be the hero of the day when he saved the resulting spot-kick to earn West Ham a point.

With the turbulent month of November drawing to a close for Spurs, club Chairman Daniel Levy revealed in an interview with *The Sun* his desire to ensure that Berbatov remained at the club for the rest of the season and beyond: 'I very much hope Dimitar will be here at the start of next season but I hope that for most of our players. It's always difficult talking about individual players when you're coming up to a transfer window. I don't expect any of our first-team players to be leaving in January and I very much hope they'll be here in the summer. But the summer is a long way off and a lot can happen between now and then. No one person is bigger than the club. This is a team.'

Back in the UEFA Cup, Juande Ramos continued his unbeaten start at Spurs when his team secured a 3-2 win at the Lane against Aalborg. However, his unbeaten run had looked to be on the verge of ending when the Danish team darted into a 2-0 lead going into the break. But after half-time a rejuvenated Spurs blasted out of the blocks with a goal just 40 seconds after the restart. Berbatov turned the ball home for his fourth goal of the campaign, following a sublime pass from substitute Tom Huddlestone who had only just entered the fray for Jenas. Berbatov then turned provider once again minutes later when his hard work allowed Keane to set up Malbranque for the equaliser. And with just over 20 minutes of the match remaining, Ramos' other half-time substitute, Darren Bent, fired home from Lennon's cross to complete a remarkable comeback and send the Spurs crowd delirious with joy.

After the thrilling comeback, Berbatov revealed to *Sky Sports News* his happiness at playing under Ramos and the confidence the new man had given the team to reinvigorate their performances on the pitch: 'He is a confident man, we can tell by the way he explains things and the way he handles things. That helps us and that gives us confidence. The results speak for themselves. We haven't lost a game since he is here so we are on the right path. Hopefully we can do that on Sunday against Birmingham, it will be fantastic for our fans as well. I am happy I play and I try to help my team.'

But Berbatov's words appeared to act as a curse, as

Ramos' unbeaten record went in the very next game with Spurs losing at home to Birmingham courtesy of a last-gasp strike from former Arsenal midfielder Sebastian Larsson, to earn Alex McCleish a win in his first game in charge of the Midlands team. Birmingham took the lead when Gary McSheffrey scored from the spot after being fouled by Kaboul. But Spurs bounced back with a penalty of their own when Berbatov was hauled down by on-loan Arsenal defender Johan Djourou to allow Keane to equalise just after half-time. Keane then put Spurs into the lead, before Cameron Jerome brought the scores level again.

However, Keane was dismissed soon after when he was adjudged to have lunged in on Birmingham midfielder Fabrice Muamba. Despite the dismissal, Spurs looked to have done enough to earn a point until Larsson popped up with his wonder goal to give Birmingham a first win at the Lane in 24 years.

Spurs bounced back from the last-gasp defeat to Birmingham to secure qualification for the knock out stages of he UEFA Cup with a 1-1 draw at against Anderlecht in Belgium, when substitute Berbatov fired home a penalty to equalise Bart Goor's opener for the team Spurs had beaten on penalties in the 1984 UEFA Cup final.

And Spurs secured a third Premier League win in their next game at home to Manchester City with Berbatov displaying his full array of skills to inspire his team-mates to victory. Firstly the Bulgarian set up an opportunity for strike partner Bent but the England international saw Andreas Isaksson prevent a certain goal when he was quick to rush off his line and clear the danger. Berbatov then somehow managed to put Bent through again despite being on the floor but once again Bent failed to take advantage of the chance when he screwed his shot wide of the post. With Berbatov outshining his national team colleague Martin Petrov for City, Spurs' inventive striker then provided Malbranque with a chance to open the scoring but this time the shot was blocked by City captain Richard Dunne.

Inevitably, Berbatov was involved in the opening goal, when he firstly won his team a free-kick and then found Chimbonda with a flick from Jenas' resultant cross to allow the Frenchman to score, albeit with the aid of his arm rather than his head to City's utter disbelief. Petrov then started to influence the game more and more and it was he who provided the cross for replacement Rolando Bianchi to head home City's equaliser. However, following Stephen Ireland's dismissal for a reckless lunge, Jermain Defoe smacked home the winner from a free-kick to seal three much-needed points for Ramos' team.

A few days after Spurs' victory over City, Berbatov spoke out in an interview with the *Daily Star* and spoke of his love and admiration for the Spurs fans for sticking by the team through thick and thin: 'It's a pleasure and an honour to play for Tottenham and I enjoy myself here. We are having a difficult time at the moment, not every day can be a good day but we must stay strong. I love everyone who loves Tottenham and I see the passion of our fans. It doesn't matter if we are winning or losing, they are still behind us and that is what I appreciate. We are not in a good position in the table. We know we should not be there and it is frustrating. I know we have a brilliant squad, with so much ability and class throughout. We are working hard to put things right and with the new boss I'm confident we are on the right track again.'

In the team's next match against Portsmouth at Fratton Park, Berbatov collected his first goal in eight league games with just 10 minutes remaining, as Spurs picked up their first away win of the league season. Berbatov had missed earlier opportunities in the match to seal the points for the visitors but when Lennon beat his man and floated in a inch-perfect cross, the Bulgarian made no mistake as he stroked the ball home with ease.

Spurs followed up their impressive win over Pompey with a third win in a row as they beat Manchester City again, this time in the Carling Cup quarter-final at Eastlands, to set up a semi-final showdown with Arsenal for the second season in a row. Spurs were reduced to 10 men for the majority of the match after Didier Zokora was dismissed for a sliding tackle on Elano, but Spurs already held a one-goal lead through Jermain Defoe and they extended their lead when Malbranque made sure of victory with a clinical late breakaway goal. And Spurs finished second in UEFA Cup Group G, after being denied top spot by Getafe, when the Spanish side secured a 2-1 home victory over Anderlecht to leave the North London club facing a last 32 tie with Slavia Prague, who they had defeated in the first round of the same competition the previous season.

Once again, with the transfer window fast approaching, Spurs reacted to rumours of renewed interest from Manchester United in Berbatov, when Damien Comolli told *Sky Sports News*: 'It's pure speculation. We never had any talks with Manchester United and as Juande Ramos has stated twice this week we want Dimitar to stay with us. For us it is not an issue. I don't think there is a price for him.'

Comolli added that Spurs also hoped to keep hold of Jermain Defoe and admitted that they could look to add players to the squad in January if the right players were to become available: 'We've stated several times that we want him to stay and he's stated that he wants to stay. When two parties want to succeed I think we are going to get an agreement. We always try to come out of the transfer window better than we enter into it. If there are opportunities we will do something.'

With the second North London derby against Arsenal looming large, Gunners boss Arsene Wenger admitted that his side would have to be wary of the threat posed by Berbatov when the two sides clashed the following weekend. Wenger said: 'It seems, especially in the last two or three games, that when Berbatov plays well, so do Tottenham. The quality of Tottenham's performances recently can be linked with the gain in form of Berbatov. His intelligence, his technique and the quality of his movement have impressed me. He is one of the Premier League's better strikers.'

And Wenger also spoke of his belief that with Ramos at the helm, Spurs could be in line to achieve some success in the future: 'I think Ramos can achieve something at Tottenham. He has the experience and plenty of resources. He has the chance to do it because

Tottenham already had a good team before he came – they have finished fifth for the last two seasons.'

The first half between the two bitter rivals remained goalless and dull as both teams struggled to take a firm stranglehold on the match. But the second half proved exhilarating as the match sparked into life just after the restart. With only two minutes on the second half clock, Fabregas played in Emmanuel Adebayor for the opener with a sumptuous backheel to put the Gunners in charge at the Emirates.

However, the lead didn't last long as Berbatov gave the travelling Spurs supporters reason to celebrate when he smashed home from a tight angle to level the scores. And soon after, Spurs fans were celebrating again when the referee pointed to the penalty spot after the Bulgarian was brought down in the area by Kolo Toure. Unfortunately for Spurs though, Keane's penalty was blocked by Manuel Almunia to keep the scores level at 1-1. Wenger then sent on Nicklas Bendtner as the home team, spurred on by Almunia's penalty save, went in search of a winner. And within seconds of his introduction, the Danish striker was celebrating scoring with his first touch when he lost his marker, Huddlestone, to head home Fabregas' corner to seal yet another win for Arsenal over their arch-rivals.

In the aftermath of the victory, Wenger praised Berbatov for an outstanding performance against his team, telling *goal.com*: 'Berbatov is a bit like Thierry. He doesn't turn up where you want him to be. Left, right, centre, he goes everywhere. He has the same temperament as Thierry, too. He shows his emotions. He was outstanding against us.'

In the following day's *News of the World*, Keane begged the Spurs hierarchy to do all in their power to retain the services of his eastern European strike partner: 'You don't want your best players going, certainly not someone like Berbatov, because we want to progress and do better. Dimitar is under contract until something changes – in that the club decide to get rid of him or he wants to go. But as far as I'm concerned he is here for a few years and that's the way it is. Berbatov is a wonderful player. He has everything to be the very best; it's just up to him. When you play with such a good striker such as Dimitar it makes your own job so much easier. He understands what I'm going to do and I understand him. It's the big man, little man partnership and so far since he's come it's worked.'

In the meantime, former head coach Martin Jol told *Sportsweek* that he believed he would have had a better chance of bringing glory to White Hart Lane if Comolli had delegated more control to him over transfers: 'From the first day it was an awkward working relationship. I was not his choice and he was not my choice. For the most important part of my job I was depending on the people around me at Spurs who were buying the players. Spurs is a fantastic club with fantastic supporters but I often think "if only I'd been allowed to run the club the way I wanted it"'

Jol continued by criticising Ramos for his admission before his appointment to the Spurs hotseat that he received a lucrative offer to take over Jol's job at White Hart Lane: 'It was not the most elegant thing to do to a colleague, making public that he had received a big offer from Tottenham. From that moment on I knew I had a massive battle with my players every day. Every day the players asked me if I was staying as a manager but I did not know the answer myself.'

Spurs bounced back to winning ways on Boxing Day after the disappointing derby-day defeat to Arsenal with a 5-1 demolition of Fulham at the Lane. Captain Ledley King provided a boost for the club when he returned to the starting lineup for his first appearance of the season as Spurs went into the half-time break leading by two goals courtesy of Keane and Huddlestone. Fulham pulled a goal back after the break but further goals from Keane, Huddlestone and a fifth from substitute Defoe wrapped up an easy victory for Spurs over their west London rivals.

And Spurs continued where they had left off against Fulham when they fired six goals past Reading to win an incredible match 6-4 at the Lane as Ramos' side continued their climb away from the relegation zone. The star of the show almost inevitably once again was Berbatov, who helped himself to four goals to guide Spurs to an important victory after they had found themselves trailing 4-3 at one point. After the match the *Daily Telegraph* quoted Ramos as begging his chairman Daniel Levy to keep hold of Berbatov, with the transfer window set to re-open: 'He made a great contribution against Reading. Magnificent! He is a very valuable player for us. But I cannot assure that he is going to stay at the club because the chairman has to decide that. The chairman knows I want Berbatov to stay. If it was up to me we would not lose him but there are different circumstances and factors that we have to take into account such as the player's opinion and feelings. If it was up to me he would continue with us.'

And Poyet marvelled at Berbatov's one-man show against Reading when he told *Sky Sports*: 'He was different class. I cannot think of another player who can do what he does every week. We don't expect him to score four every week but he is capable of doing anything on the pitch. To score four two days before the window opens I am sure there are going to be even more rumours from now on, but I'm just looking forward to him staying for the rest of the season.'

But Poyet also revealed that despite Berbatov's virtuoso performance the coaching staff would have to get back to work on the defensive side of the team's game immediately after conceding, when he said: 'We have to put it [the defence] right as soon as possible. We need to make sure we do not need to score six every game. We have to be solid because the quality in front of goal is there. It was a fantastic game for the supporters, very entertaining, but it was not a good game for the managers. But we got the three points and we said before the game against Fulham that we needed to win these two games.'

Berbatov agreed with Poyet's assessment of the performance and told *The Guardian*: 'In the end we must look over the mistakes we allowed to be scored against us. We conceded easy goals from free-kicks and corners and that's not good because we keep doing that in every game. We've shown our qualities many times but we also show how bad we can be sometimes. We must cut that out. I go home and keep running the game over in my head, thinking about what I and the team can do better. I hope everybody does this because that's the way to improve.'

Spurs managed to sew up their first piece of business early in the transfer window when they completed the signing of Cardiff City's highly-rated defender Chris Gunter. And with the club being linked with a move for Ajax defender Urby Emanuelson, and striker Darren Bent with a move away from White Hart Lane, Levy told the club website: 'Juande, Damien and I have reviewed the squad and Juande feels that we are not looking at any major changes. We are all clear that the January window is the worst time to buy quality players so we shall not be doing any business that is not essential. Once again for the record, we are not a selling club, rather we are building for the future. When we have players on long contracts we have no need to entertain offers.'

And Ramos reiterated his chairman's sentiments that Berbatov would be going nowhere when he told the *Daily Telegraph*: 'Berbatov is not for sale and we don't want to sell him. This is the contractual situation at the moment. There is no offer on the table for him to leave. We have four strikers and we are very happy with them. We have to try to take advantage of them and make sure they work well together and gel well with the rest of the team.'

With Berbatov being heavily linked to a possible exit away from Spurs in virtually every newspaper, *The Express* writer John Dillon told Sky Sports' *Sunday Supplement* programme: 'Teams are attempting to break into the top four, but this is the sort of thing they are coming up against. Berbatov's a great player and he scored four goals yesterday. Tottenham have been through a big upheaval and brought in a new manager with the idea being that he is going to get them into the top four. But it defeats the object of the exercise if they then sell this great player to get their hands on the huge amount of money that is available.

'What are they going to do with it? They've only got to spend it on another player. It's a bit like the housing market in a way. But at the same time it's difficult to keep a player that is unhappy. A player's head is going to be turned if he finds out Manchester United wants him. It shows that shift in where the power of the game lies. A successful Tottenham team playing great attacking football is a great part of the tradition of the game, and yet a guy like this doesn't consider it a big enough stage for him any more. It's utterly ridiculous.'

And the *Daily Mail*'s Paul Hayward agreed with Dillon's comments, saying: 'It would be a shame if he left. As I understand it he was very nearly sold to Manchester United in the summer and they thought he was leaving then. They clearly think he is leaving now because the manager has said he can't guarantee he will stay. I think he's a wonderful player, but he disappointed me earlier in the season with his demeanour. I thought he was in a sulk quite a lot of the time, which is unbecoming of a great player. But maybe he just feels he doesn't want to be there. Ironically though Tottenham are starting to pick up now and are starting to look like a good team again. There is a good reason for him to stay and stick it out there. But maybe behind the scenes he has been made an offer that he can't resist.'

Meanwhile, despite Ramos and Levy's declaration that Berbatov would be going nowhere in the transfer window, the Bulgarian's agent Emil Dantchev appeared to be preparing his client for a move away from Spurs when he was reported to have told *The Sun*: 'I have already spoken to the Tottenham chairman Daniel Levy and told him that if a club which corresponds to Dimitar's class and ambition comes in with an offer which suits his current club in January, he would like to be allowed to go. I would like to stress this is not about money, this is about sporting ambition, nor has it anything to do with the new manager Juande Ramos. Dimitar is perfectly happy with Ramos and the way he is working but after Tottenham's bad start to the season it is unlikely they will have the chance to do something big this season.'

Dantchev added: 'Dimitar is OK at Tottenham. I would not say he is happy but his performances for the club are a testament to his commitment to the fans and his team-mates. He has never stopped trying and scoring goals to help the team. Fans must understand Dimitar is 27 next month and time is running out for him to play for a club which can match his ambition. It is a long-term plan for Spurs. Dimitar wants to fulfil his potential and win trophies now. He would definitely consider a move outside of England. That is not the issue. What matters is a club which matches his ambition and his level, and therefore there are only five or six around Europe. Two clubs outside of England and one from the Premier League are interested in him.'

The team began 2008 with a disappointing 2-1 defeat in the Midlands at the hands of Aston Villa, as goals from Olof Mellberg and Martin Laursen took the Villans up to sixth position in the league table, while Spurs struggled to recapture the deadly attacking play which had seen them score 11 goals in their last two matches.

After the match, Ramos admitted his disappointment at the result, and hinted that the club could be on the lookout for defenders: 'I am not happy because we have come back from a goal down, created chances, and still lost. I think a draw would have been a fairer result. But in the past few weeks, we have conceded goals from set-pieces, and it is hard to win matches conceding as many as we do from those sort of positions. We are lacking in some defensive departments, and it is something we need to look at. We are paying for lapses. We need to find a solution to our defensive problems. If we can't sort the problems out with the players we already have here, we will look outside for other players.'

And speaking once again on the constant rumours about Berbatov's future and his agent's comments that his client could be set to move on, Ramos said: 'Obviously Berbatov's agent is looking to do his business and has made his comments. But we are happy because we have the player on a contract, and we plan to keep him.'

Meanwhile, Gus Poyet revealed to the joy of the supporters, that the club had yet to receive an offer for Berbatov: 'There is nothing on the table and there is nothing happening. It is not a problem for us. We are happy with Berba, he is here and it is no drama. We want to improve and we want to go to a better level – he has to stay.'

And with the speculation over Berbatov's future reaching fever pitch, with Chelsea, AC Milan and Manchester United rumoured to be trailing him, Ramos told *Sky Sports* that it was his belief that any club wanting to make Berbatov an offer would need to break the British transfer record of £31 million paid by Chelsea for Andriy Shevchenko, to prize their leading scorer away from White Hart Lane.

'I think a club would have to break the British transfer record to sign Berbatov', he said. 'It's normal that they would have to pay such an amount. There are very few players of his class. At this moment Berbatov's value is more than this price. At least that is what we think. But everyone has a price. The intention of Tottenham is not to sell the player. It's not a question for me if a club can pay this. The other clubs will know what they need for their squads.

'Unless something strange happens – and I think it will not happen – there's not going to be a club that will pay the price that Tottenham could accept. The truth is that I understand perfectly why he would cost so much money because there are few players like Berbatov. And those who do exist play for great teams who play in the Champions League. And those great teams will not sell their players. He's the only great player who has not played in the Champions League that they could sign.

'I fully expect that at the end of January I will have all my four strikers. At this moment I am convinced they will continue with us because we want them to. But from the first moment the decision has been out of my hands. The final decision rests with the club. I don't want to sell Berbatov. I want the best players – but the club have to make a decision.'

Goalkeeper Paul Robinson also came out in the press and revealed his own hopes that Spurs could hold on to Berbatov throughout the transfer window, stating that the club had to strive to keep hold of their best players in order to build for the future:

'Obviously you see the speculation, but until there is any substance we just laugh it off and wind him up at the moment. If there is any substance to it, we will have to wait and see. Dimitar is a fantastic player and a top talent and, if we want to be going the right way, we need to keep players such as Berbatov. I think Tottenham is a big club. Hopefully we can get to the Carling Cup final this year and hopefully with a new manager we can build on results and start climbing the table as well. We are making progress, it is slow progress but we are going the right way up the table. You look where we were when the manager first took over and it was disappointing for everybody but we are moving in the right direction. There is still a long way to go in the season. I feel the team's performances have picked up and hopefully, with a little bit of luck, and a little bit of organisation, cutting out silly mistakes, we will get results.'

Speaking to the *Daily Mail* about his international colleague's situation, Aston Villa midfielder Stilian Petrov revealed that in his opinion he could foresee Berbatov making a move to one of the big clubs trailing his signature and that Spurs would face a fight to persuade him to stay at White Hart Lane.

'Dimitar is a very ambitious guy and he will get what he wants because he is top quality, a world-class player', said Petrov. 'The last two seasons he has been very dangerous. I'm not surprised that the big teams are looking at him. I hope he fulfils his ambitions. Obviously, he also wants to be happy and I hope that he will be when everything is all over. He is under a lot of pressure right now to score goals and all of a sudden there is this saga over whether he is going to leave. That affects a player out on the pitch. So it is important for him to be happy. I know he will make the right decision for him.'

However, Ramos responded to the speculation by telling *The Guardian* that Spurs were looking to hold on to all their top players: 'I think Tottenham is a perfect team for him. We are in a phase of growth and of course we don't want to sell him because we want to keep our best players. When we get the chance we will try and improve the team by signing players of his level so that the level of the team increases as much as possible. I have spoken to Dimitar and he tells me he is happy to stay here. I hope he will.'

Following a week in which the Bulgarian's future had dominated the back pages of the British newspapers, Berbatov got back to concentrating on playing football as Spurs' let a 2-1 lead slip at the Lane as Reading fought back to claim a 2-2 FA Cup third round draw. Berbatov helped himself to another two goals to add to his season's tally, including one from the penalty spot and his influence on the game saw him draw further praise from his manager Ramos: 'He's a professional. He's done everything he could and collaborated with his goals. He's had a very good game today.'

Just a week into January and Berbatov had had enough of all the conjecture regarding his next destination. Would it be Manchester? Would it be Milan? Would it be West London and Chelsea? Or would he move anywhere? The forward spoke to Bulgarian television station *Nova tv* and revealed that his aim was to remain at the Lane and help Spurs win titles and silverware:

'There are too many speculations around my name, but most of them are foolish. It's absurd and I'm tired of seeing my name in the newspapers. I want to live in peace. It is getting too much. I am a Tottenham player and I'm trying to give my best, so I can help my team. I'm happy when we play well and I'm miserable when we lose our games. I'm happy at the moment. You can win titles and medals with every team and I can win with Tottenham too.'

And commenting on the rumour that Spurs had placed a £31 million price tag on his head in an attempt to ward off potential suitors, Berbatov declared his surprise saying: 'It's ridiculous. I don't think that I'm worth so much money. I just have to do my job and score goals. I'm not a one-man team. Everybody in the team supports me and I've never heard a reproach or felt envy. Juande is very good, both as a man and as a coach. He sees even the small details that remain hidden from most people.'

With a massive Carling Cup tie awaiting with bitter rivals Arsenal, Spurs' fit-again captain Ledley King revealed that the team were determined to make amends for the disappointment of losing out the previous season at the semi-final stage to the same opposition:

'It was one of our biggest disappointments. We are hungry to put that right and we are happy we have got the chance to play them again. We have learnt a lot from last season's disappointment and we will be stronger this time around. There are new players in, the manager has changed, but the core of the team is still the same. Having got to the semi-final, we want to go on and win it, but Arsenal can score from anywhere. We know that against a side like Arsenal, we can't afford to make many mistakes so that will be in our plans when we go to the Emirates on Wednesday. We will want to stay solid because we know we can score goals.'

And King stated before the match that he was in agreement with the various factions calling for the club's hierarchy to retain the Bulgarian's services: 'It's no surprise he is being linked [with a move] away but we want to keep hold of our best players. If we want to be moving in the right direction, we need to hold on to him, it's as simple as that.'

Meanwhile, despite his client's public admission that he intended to remain at White Hart Lane for the foreseeable future, and Spurs' insistence that they wanted to build a team strong enough to constantly challenge for silverware, his agent Emil Dantchev, had other ideas. Somewhat surprisingly, he told *Sky Sports News* that he stood by his previous comments which suggested the Bulgarian captain himself had admitted he would consider his position if a bigger club came in for him in the transfer window. Dantchev said: 'I am not a liar. The position I stressed is not my position, it is the position of the player. Berbatov wants to know his position directly at a press conference organised by his club, if they decide to do this. The one thing Berbatov needs is to live his life, and be able to do his job for his club.'

Ahead of the semi-final first leg clash between the two North London giants at the Emirates, Arsenal boss Arsene Wenger admitted to the club's official website that he had considered making a move for Berbatov while the striker was still at Leverkusen, but decided against the move due an embarrassment of riches in the forward area. Wenger said: 'He is top class. He always has time on the pitch and when you play against him he is always in the places you don't want him to be. He is what I call a top class striker because he can provide, he can score, he can be at the start of the move and at the end of it. That is a sign of quality.

'When he played for Bayer Leverkusen I noticed him once when he played against Real Madrid. He was a young boy at the time, but we were never in need of him. We had Thierry Henry, we had Robin van Persie. Then we got (Emmanuel) Adebayor, but I have known about him for a long time. I always look more at the individual quality of a player first and Berbatov had top technical quality, he is tall, in England it helps.'

With Berbatov's future still up in the air one player potentially on his way out of Spurs was Jermain Defoe, who was advised by the club's hierarchy that he was free to leave the club if a suitable offer came in. And although Wenger was linked in some newspapers with what would be a highly-contentious move to take the pocket-sized goalscorer across North London to the Emirates, the Arsenal boos refuted the rumours vehemently: 'Up front we have Bendtner, Eduardo, Van Persie and of course we have Adebayor. Walcott can play there too. Then we have Carlos Vela don't forget for next season. At the moment we are not interested in any other strikers.'

The first leg of the semi-final proved to be a close match as Spurs went in search of a decent result to take back to the Lane for the return leg two weeks later. With Berbatov and Keane's creativity causing 'Wenger's kids' no end of trouble at the top end of the pitch, Spurs looked the more likely team to open the scoring as Jamie O'Hara, Malbranque and the Bulgarian striker himself went close to grabbing the first goal of a keenly contested match. But the first goal wasn't too long coming. Berbatov picked up the ball following a weak defensive header by Johan Djourou to chip the ball through for Keane, who in turn squared a pass for Jenas to fire home past Lukas Fabianski in the Arsenal goal. It gave the visitors a deserved half-time lead and the Spurs supporters inside the ground reason to dream of a first trip to Wembley since 1999.

But Arsenal didn't give in and dragged themselves level with only 11 minutes of the match remaining when a sliding tackle from the South Korean left back Young-Pyo Lee deflected onto Theo Walcott, who had broken forward, and looped over a helpless Radek Cerny in the Spurs goal. The match ended 1-1 but Spurs could have taken a 2-1 lead back to the Lane ahead of the second leg if Defoe, on as a substitute, could have kept his shot down when given a golden opportunity to win the game.

Spurs followed up the draw at Arsenal with a disappointing 2-0 league defeat away at the hands of Avram Grant's Chelsea, but the team picked themselves up to progress to the fourth round of the FA Cup and a clash with Manchester United at Old Trafford, after beating Reading 1-0 at the Madejski. Goals from Aaron Lennon and Keane then ensured Spurs took maximum points from their game with Roy Keane's struggling Sunderland team at the Lane. Ramos' men warmed up for the midweek semi-final second leg of the Carling Cup with Arsenal with a comfortable victory to continue the club's climb away from the bottom end of the Premier League table.

And as the excitement around the streets of North London began to build in the run up to the decisive second leg, Ramos told *The Express* that progression to the final at the expense of their great rivals could be a deciding factor in persuading Berbatov to commit his long-term future to Spurs: 'If we manage to get through and advance to the higher echelons of competitions and get to finals, then Dimitar will get chances on the world stage he deserves. That is what the club need to do to keep him and that is what we're working on.'

However, Berbatov's agent Dantchev continued to suggest that his client remaining at the Lane was not the forgone conclusion many believed it to now be, when he said: 'There are 10 days until the end of the transfer window, then everybody will know where he will be.'

And so, the Spurs players ran out at White Hart Lane to a firecracker atmosphere with the prize of a place in the Carling Cup final up for grabs, and almost as importantly the chance to secure the bragging rights until the 2008–09 season as the rivals prepared to face one another for the fourth and final time of the season.

Spurs flew out of the starting blocks as if possessed and within three minutes of the game kicking off, Jenas latched onto a through ball from Berbatov before sidestepping Justin Hoyte and calmly stroking home the opening goal to send the home supporters wild with delight. And things got even better in the 26th minute when Nicklas Bendtner diverted a free-kick from Jenas into his own net to leave Arsenal chasing the game. Enjoying a two-goal cushion, Spurs began to play some really slick football and Berbatov almost increased the lead further, only to see his shot rebound off the base of Fabianski's post, as Spurs took a two-goal lead in at half-time.

Mindful that they had allowed a two-goal advantage to slip the season before to Arsenal in the semi-final, before losing the second leg, Spurs came out after the break in search of a killer third goal and they didn't have long to wait for it when Keane rifled home a half-volley following some intricate play from Lennon to give Spurs an almost unassailable 3-0 lead.

Lennon scored a fourth to settle the match and further enhance the bubbling atmosphere within the Lane, and although Arsenal pulled a goal back, Malbranque added a fifth in stoppage time to ensure it would be a night that no Spurs fan would ever forget. The team kept on course to finally win some silverware for the first time in nine long years.

Berbatov spoke of his joy at helping the team reach a final after a difficult opening to the season in an interview with the *Daily Telegraph*: 'The performance against Arsenal was magnificent. The way we played and the way we supported each other, that's what I want to see. It doesn't matter who scored the goals, in the end the victory is important. We showed that if we play like that we have a great future. We showed what we are capable of against a very good Arsenal team with great players. We were above them and wanted the win more than they did and we achieved it.'

He added: 'I have never played at Wembley before and everybody is excited. Wembley is a legendary stadium and I am looking forward to playing there. I have always wanted to go there and watch a game, but it's another thing to go there and play. There are no words to describe the noise and the atmosphere against Arsenal. In the end, we did it for every fan of Tottenham. Now let's hope we can do it again for them at Wembley.

'I know we can achieve a lot. Sometimes we underestimate our ability to do great things. But this is an example of what we can achieve against a great opponent. We showed that this club can challenge for trophies. If we believe in our quality it doesn't matter who we play, we have great players and we have a coach who can achieve a lot with us. Let's all believe in Tottenham and we won't disappoint anyone.'

And shifting the praise for the victory onto the shoulders of Ramos, Berbatov added: 'I'm not surprised how quickly the manager has turned things around because he is a great coach. He proved himself in Spain and now he is here. The way he talks with us and worked with us, we see we can go places.'

Ramos responded by praising the effort, commitment and desire shown by the team to win through to the final in such style, and also revealed his happiness for the long-suffering Spurs faithful who continually support they team through thick and thin:

'It is a fantastic achievement. It's been a long time since the fans have had the flavour of a final. That makes it all the more satisfying. There have been big changes. But without the collaboration of the footballers themselves, this would have been impossible. The huge effort the players have made to come out of a bad situation means we have been improving. They are the architects of this change.

'There is great satisfaction in beating a club like Arsenal, first because they are such great rivals, and then because we hadn't beaten them for so long. Add to that the scoreline...it's all the more satisfying. It was the most complete game my side has played since I came here. We didn't make mistakes and were perfect in all areas of the pitch. The effort that the players have put in to reach this final means so much.'

And the Spaniard continued: 'Going to Wembley is like a religious experience, a mythical venue in the home of football. If you get to Wembley as a coach or a player then it's like getting a PhD or being knighted, in football terms, like nothing you could experience anywhere else in the world. Beating Arsenal like that in front of our own supporters was like a final for us. It's always been my aim to make big impacts in cup competitions because when I arrived there was no possibility of winning the league. The change has been enormous in the short time the players and my staff have been together. I arrived to a depressed bunch and you could see from how often their leads were overhauled that they didn't believe in themselves. But we are talking about a total transformation. Against Arsenal we scored five and could easily have scored many more. It was one of those games where every detail you draw on the blackboard in the team talks came off. But the key thing is the players now believe in themselves – we've won back our pride and aggression.'

With only one week of the transfer window remaining for players to be brought in or sold by club's throughout Europe, Ramos admitted in an interview with Spanish magazine *AS* that he was still nervous despite the club reaching the Carling Cup final just days before that somebody would make a last-ditch move for his star performer Berbatov: 'We count on him, but while the market is still open there is always a risk because he is a great player and it is normal that there is interest. But he is happy and is enjoying playing for the team so, it would have to be an offer from a very big club, with a very big contract to make him leave.'

With progression to one final already assured, Spurs travelled north to face Manchester United in the fourth round of the FA Cup just days after the Arsenal game looking to keep their chances of reaching the final of the other major domestic cup alive. And with Spurs' five-star performance against Arsenal fresh in the memory, United manager Sir Alex Ferguson admitted in the *Daily Telegraph* in the build up to the game that his players would need to be aware of the threat posed by Ramos' in-form striker, Berbatov: 'Berbatov to me, without doubt, has been fantastic since he arrived from Bayer Leverkusen. He is a good player. He is a big strong, lad too. He is well-balanced and hard to shake off the ball.'

But on the day, despite some nice touches and a few chances for Berbatov to get his name on the scoresheet, it was Ferguson's own in-form forward, Cristiano Ronaldo, who struck twice to inspire United to a 3-1 victory. Berbatov almost opened the scoring in the 16th minute with a header, only to see United striker Wayne Rooney clear the goalbound effort off the line. Spurs did take the lead after 24 minutes when Lennon's trickery set up Keane to fire past Edwin van der Sar in the United goal.

Carlos Tevez grabbed an equaliser shortly before half-time and a penalty from Ronaldo put United in front midway though the second half. Spurs thought they had grabbed a deserved equaliser in the 85th minute only to see Berbatov's effort rebound off the post, before Ronaldo ensured it would be United who would progress with his second of the match late on.

Ramos moved to bring in three defenders before the closure of the transfer window on 31 January 2008. Jonathan Woodgate from Middlesbrough, Alan Hutton from Rangers and left back Gilberto from Hertha Berlin were all recruited as Ramos sought to try and shore up his team's leaky defence. And the Spaniard also found himself linked with moves to bring in Valencia's deposed captain David Albelda and Middlesbrough's England winger Stewart Downing. However, the three defenders proved to be Ramos' only late dealings in the market, while the window came and went with Berbatov remaining a Spurs player.

Berbatov revealed his absolute delight at the closure of the window to *Sky Sports News*, suggesting that he hoped it would bring to a halt, the continuous and unsettling speculation that had followed his every move throughout January: 'Who knows what the future holds? I don't know. I am happy at Tottenham, at the moment. I am happy that the speculation is over, now that the transfer window has closed. I can now concentrate fully on my game. Sometimes all this talk and rumours mess with your head. Yes [it may have affected my game during January]. Sometimes you just want to be left alone so you can play your game. But it is over now.'

One player who did depart White Hart Lane however was Jermain Defoe who packed his bags and headed for the south coast and Harry Redknapp's Portsmouth. Speaking about the deadline day move, Berbatov admitted that it had come as something of a surprise to him: 'I was surprised. I was under the impression that he was going to stay with us. But in the last moment of the transfer window, he was gone. I wish him all the best because he is a great talent and it was a pleasure to work with him.'

And so with his immediate short term future tied to Spurs and the opportunity to go to Wembley and win only a second winners' medal of his career to look forward to things were looking up for the Bulgarian after his less than auspicious start to the season. With the team also progressing nicely in the UEFA Cup, the chances of obtaining more silverware that season was also a realistic possibility. But first it was time for Berba to take his bow and make his mark at Wembley.

CHAPTER 11

GLORY GLORY TOTTENHAM HOTSPUR

'I want to win things and hopefully this is the first of many for me.'
BERBATOV ON 2008 CARLING CUP

Tottenham's epic victory over Arsenal in the Carling Cup semi-final ensured that the club and their passionate and loyal fans would enjoy a first trip down Wembley Way in nine years, where they would face another of their biggest rivals in the final, Chelsea. The reigning League Cup holders from west London had themselves beaten off the stubborn challenge of Everton to reach the final and were certain to provide stern resistance to Tottenham's chances of winning their first trophy since 1999.

Allan Nielsen, the tenacious Danish international midfielder, had been the hero on that momentous occasion, when his solitary strike proved sufficient to see off the challenge of Leicester City and give George Graham's outfit the trophy in the penultimate final to be held at Wembley before the grand old stadium's closure for reconstruction. Three years later the club had progressed to the final once again – held at Cardiff's Millennium Stadium with Wembley out of action – but Blackburn Rovers had spoilt the party on that day with a 2-1 victory.

Spurs entered the 2008 showpiece as underdogs in the opinion of the majority of bookmakers, but with a strike force of Keane and Berbatov worthy of causing any team problems and a defence strengthened by the arrivals of Jonathan Woodgate and Alan Hutton and further boosted by the timely return of skipper Ledley King, Juande Ramos's men entered the match confident of bringing the cup back to North London. A long-awaited cup-in-hand victory parade down the Tottenham High Road would be the prize.

In the countdown to the final, Berbatov had been in fine scoring form, notching up a goal against Manchester United at the Lane in a game Spurs were unfortunate not to win after conceding a very late equaliser and also in the straight forward 3-0 away win over Derby County and the first leg of the UEFA Cup win over Slavia Prague. With progression to the last 16 of the UEFA Cup secured following a 1-1 draw with Slavia in the return leg at the Lane, Ramos revealed how much he wanted the team to win the cup for Spurs loyal and passionate fans, but also how tough it would be to do so, saying: 'We know Chelsea are good and probably go into the final as favourites because they are higher up in the league table as us. But every game is different and anything can happen in football. It would be absolutely magnificent to win a cup; it would bring tremendous happiness to the club – who need a trophy.'

Meanwhile, a number of pundits singled out Spur's deadly strike force as a potential difference between the two teams ahead of the final. *Sky Sports'* former Spurs captain, Jamie Redknapp, was adamant that for Spurs to take the trophy back to north London, Keane and Berbatov would have perform at their very best: 'The partnership of Dimitar Berbatov and Robbie Keane will need to continue its fine form. They're really important for Ramos. Berbatov is capable of doing something different – he can put that bit of stardust on the pitch with his imagination, great touch and his eye for goal. He's sorted out his problems. Earlier in the season he was more a hindrance than a help, but now he's getting on with his game and playing well. I'm also a big Robbie Keane fan and I think they make a great partnership.'

And the front pairing of Keane and Berbatov was also occupying the thoughts of the man entrusted with keeping the prolific duo off the score sheet. Chelsea goalkeeper Petr Cech admitted Keane and Berbatov – who had already notched 36 goals between them for the season before kick-off – would pose the biggest threat to his team, saying: 'I think one of their biggest strengths is Berbatov with Keane and the movement. They always find the space that is uncomfortable for defenders. With the quality they have they can make a difference, but without good supply they cannot play on their own, so I think they need [Steed] Malbranque, [Jermaine] Jenas and the others to give them good balls. If you don't allow their midfield to pass the ball, or allow Berbatov and Keane space, that will be the key.'

Another former fans' favourite, David Ginola, also

singled out Berbatov as the potential match-winner ahead of the clash, comparing his own unique style of play to that of the Bulgarian: 'You know, what is strange, we are not the same type of players but we have similarities. We look lazy but we are not. When I say lazy, I mean when you are easy with the ball – when everything seems familiar and easy – when you control the ball, pass the ball when you dribble.

'Berbatov ... is very good in the air, he can strike the ball, he's very clever so he can pass the ball and strike the ball in situations you don't even think about. That's what makes the difference in the game ... That's the main reason why I love this game; it's about flair, about players who can make the difference without forgetting that they need other players who can do different things.'

For Berbatov the occasion would mark his first appearance in a cup final since the disappointment of losing the Champions League with Bayer Leverkusen at the final hurdle to Real Madrid in 2002. The only winner's medal of his career had been won in 1999 when he helped CSKA Sofia beat Litex Lovetch in the final of the Bulgarian Cup, the same year Spurs had won their last silverware. This was his chance to add a long-awaited team medal to a cabinet that bulged with personal accolades and player of the year medals, but only a single team winner's medal. Before kick-off, fellow striker Keane paid tribute to his Bulgarian strike partner, comparing his style of play to that of Manchester United legend Eric Cantona in an interview with the *Daily Mirror*:

'Dimi has that style in the way that he plays. To be

mentioned in the same breath of Cantona – phew! That is something as he was the best around. But Berba has that style of Cantona. We complement each other with how we play. We read each other quite well. I don't like talking about it. I prefer other people to talk about it. But so far it has been going well. Tall players are usually target men, but he has everything. He can go short, long, he holds it well, can see a pass and his assists are unbelievable. His all-round game is a different class.'

Over 30,000 expectant Spurs fans excitedly crammed into Wembley for the first Carling Cup Final to be contested at the venue since the reconstruction of the famous old stadium had been completed in 2007. The match itself would also mark only the second all-London final since the tournament's inception 48 years earlier – the first having occurred in 2007 when Chelsea defeated Arsenal in Cardiff. Spurs supporters were up for the game from the start. They chanted and sang vociferously and with a passion that overpowered any noise emanating from the Chelsea section at the opposite end of the ground.

Meanwhile, Spurs manager Juande Ramos retained Paul Robinson – who had returned at the expense of Radek Cerny for the second leg of the UEFA Cup tie with Slavia Prague the previous Thursday night – in goal as he went for his strongest available starting line-up. Woodgate partnered King in the centre of the defence, only weeks after joining the club from Middlesbrough, while Alan Hutton took the right back slot with Pascal Chimbonda deployed at left back in the absence of the injured Gareth Bale and Gilberto.

After all the pre-match formalities had been completed – the handshakes, the ritual national anthem, the team photos – referee Mark Halsey's whistle signalled the start of the match. Spurs made their intentions clear from the first whistle when Keane went close after seizing on a mistake from Chelsea right-back Juliano Belletti. John Terry got in the way to block his goal bound shot after only 30 seconds of play, but Spurs had signalled their desire to attack and take the game to the holders.

Spurs could have taken the lead twice soon after, when Chimbonda's header looped onto the crossbar, before Berbatov was unable to head home Keane's perfect cross with the goal at his mercy. With Spurs squandering chances to go in front, Chelsea made them pay when Didier Drogba fired home a dubious-looking free kick award from 20-yards out. Chelsea, the renowned masters of holding onto a one-goal lead rarely looked threatened by the Spurs attack. They huffed and puffed but were struggling to penetrate a defence orchestrated by Terry and Ricardo Carvalho.

But, with only 20 minutes remaining, Aaron Lennon, who had switched from the right to the left wing in search of more freedom, flighted a dangerous ball into the area towards substitute Tom Huddlestone, who tussled with Chelsea left-back Wayne Bridge for the ball. As the ball bounced up, Bridge handled and the alert linesman flagged for a penalty to the delight of the Spurs fans behind him. Despite Chelsea's protests, Halsey remained firm. Spurs had a golden chance to grab a deserved equaliser and turn the game on its head.

Who would take the resultant penalty? Without any hesitation Berbatov grabbed the ball. It was his time to partly exorcise the demons of 2002 when he had narrowly missed out on three winners' medals with Leverkusen. This was his moment. Taking his time in his own inimitable style, the Bulgarian remained the coolest person in the stadium, as he ambled up to the ball, eyes fixed solely on Petr Cech and rolled the ball into the net, sending the giant goalkeeper the wrong way as if he was on the training ground.

In tucking away the penalty, Berbatov became only the second Bulgarian in history to have scored a goal at either the old or rebuilt Wembley, the first having been way back in 1968 when Georgi Asparukhov – regarded by many to be among Bulgaria's greatest ever players – scored against England.

The Lilywhites' faithful went crazy as the noise levels erupted and reached fever pitch in the Spurs section of the ground. Their dream of winning a trophy at last was back on. Boosted by the goal, Spurs could smell a winner and when Zokora burst clear of the static Chelsea defence with only Cech standing between him and the goal, it seemed this was the moment. But unfortunately for Zokora – who had Berbatov in support and in an equally good position to score – he struck his shot straight at the Chelsea keeper who parried it back to him, only to see his second attempt fly wide. Zokora knew he had missed a glorious opportunity to settle the match and prevent the need for the impending extra time. With the minutes ticking away, a sublime turn and shot from Berbatov could also have won the game, if only he had

had the time to direct his shot anywhere other than straight at Cech.

With only four minutes of the 30 additional minutes played, Spurs won a free kick deep in Chelsea's half which Jermaine Jenas flighted into the heart of the opposition area. Cech appeared to be in complete control of the situation as the in-swinging free kick approached his grasp. But an inexplicable flap at the ball resulted in him pushing it against the on-rushing Woodgate, who seemingly unaware of what had just occurred, galloped away in delight as he watched the ball trickle into the empty net. His first goal in two years – when he scored for Real Madrid – and his first for Spurs sent the north London club's supporters into delirium and their west London neighbours fans into despair. Were Spurs about to put nine years of heartache and underachievement behind them?

With the score standing at 2-1 in Tottenham's favour, Chelsea pressed as the end of extra time approached, but Spurs clung on despite two late half-chances thanks to an immense rearguard action led by Ledley King and Woodgate to end the long wait for silverware. Cue party time in north London. Spurs had won the cup for the fourth time in their history and Juande Ramos, who had only been in the job for four months, upheld his record of never losing a cup final as a manager. And, for the first time since 2004, when Middlesbrough triumphed in the same competition, the big four – Manchester United, Chelsea, Arsenal and Liverpool – had missed out on one of the domestic trophies on offer.

After the match a jubilant Berbatov told Bulgarian

website gong.bg of his delight at scoring a goal at Wembley and finally getting his hands on the second winners' medal of his career after a lengthy nine year wait: 'It is a great honour to play at such a legendary stadium and I am proud to be one of the two Bulgarians to score a goal there. I am very tired right now. We played against a world-class team and I feel exhausted but extremely happy. I hope all Bulgarians are also proud of what I showed at Wembley.'

And the celebrations continued long into the night for the euphoric Spurs fans as the pubs around north London welcomed them home from their big day out at Wembley. In the aftermath of the victory, Berbatov brought further music to the ears of delighted fans when he declared his intention to remain in north London for the foreseeable future under the guidance of the impressive Ramos.

'I am here,' he said. 'I want to win things and hopefully this is the first of many for me. It means a lot to beat Chelsea. They are a fantastic team. When the final whistle blew it was an incredible feeling. Everyone was happy and it was great to see so many smiles. It's a major trophy and we wanted European football again. This is our moment, but on Tuesday we start again. We have important games ahead of us. We have big goals ahead of us. The manager is a winner and he knows how to win things. This is his first trophy and I hope it's the first of many.'

Assistant manager Gus Poyet – who played for both Spurs and Chelsea during his career as a player in England – also expressed his confidence Berbatov would remain at the club and help them achieve further success: 'I'm sure Berba is going to be here and going to be trying to win even more. He knows he can win things at this club. It was something that was difficult before, but he's now done it. There were a few players that there were rumours that they were leaving. They stayed and there were a few players that came here in January. I know that all of them now know they made the right decision, because they are already champions.'

The Carling Cup Final of 2008 will live long in the memory of Dimitar Ivanov Berbatov. And after witnessing their team overcome the odds to beat overwhelming favourites Chelsea, those supporters who were lucky enough to get a ticket to the game and the many thousands the world over who had to settle for watching it in front of the television, collectively hoped that upon the arrival of the summer transfer window of 2008, their newest idol would reject any overtures that came his way to fire their beloved Lilywhites to further magnificent days and nights of glory and silverware.

On the back of the previous weekend's glorious celebrations at the New Wembley, Ramos' men followed up their cup triumph with a trip to the Midlands to face Birmingham City with the team looking to get their preparations for the first leg of their UEFA Cup last 16 tie with PSV Eindhoven off to the best possible start. However, an inspired hat-trick from City's Finnish striker Mikael Forssell brought Spurs crashing back to earth with an almighty bump as they returned home on the back of a 4-1 hiding.

And there was to be further disappointment for the

club when a 1-0 defeat at the Lane to PSV courtesy of Jefferson Farfan's solitary away goal meant Spurs would face the uphill task of travelling to Holland a week later needing to score at least one goal to have a chance of progressing to the quarter-finals of European football's second biggest club competition.

Spurs warmed up for their vital trip to Eindhoven with a thrilling and resounding 4-0 win over London rivals West Ham at the Lane, the team's first victory since the Carling Cup triumph. Berbatov got the rout under way with a header after just seven minutes from a pinpoint Tom Huddlestone free-kick, before the same duo combined again from another set-piece to allow the deadly Bulgarian to double Spurs' advantage with another outstanding header, his sixth goal in eight matches. The big striker nearly completed his hat-trick before half-time when he latched onto yet another precise dead ball from the excellent Huddlestone, but this time West Ham goalkeeper Robert Green was able to turn his effort away. Recent arrival Gilberto came off the bench to add a third before Berbatov rattled Green's side netting as he searched in vain for his treble. Finally, another substitute, this time Darren Bent, rounded off an impressive derby victory with a late header to send Spurs and their optimistic fans on their way to Eindhoven in confident mood.

And from the kick-off in a bubbling Philips Stadion in Eindhoven, Ramos sent his team out with a mission to attack to try turn around the first leg deficit. But despite going close to finding the vital goal which would square up the tie on aggregate, it would take until the 81st minute for Spurs to break the deadlock. And once again the Spurs fans would be indebted to their star player to rescue their hopes of progressing in the competition, when the flamboyant Berbatov volleyed home Pascal Chimbonda's cross exquisitely from the edge of the box to send the tie into 30 nerve-filled minutes of extra time. The Bulgarian almost teed up Bent for a vital second away goal as extra time got under way only for the England forward to fire his shot wide. And Berbatov spurned a difficult opportunity of his own to prevent the lottery of a penalty shoot-out, when his volley on the turn flew over the bar. With the two teams inseparable after 210 minutes of football, it would indeed take a shoot-out to decide the winner of the tie.

And when Paul Robinson denied PSV striker Danko Lazovic and no other misses were registered, midfielder Jermaine Jenas shouldered the responsibility of firing Spurs into the quarter-final draw. However, Heurelho Gomes came to PSV's rescue with an outstanding save and after three further successful kicks in sudden death the unfortunate Chimbonda watched in horror as his kick skewed wide of the post to mark an end to Ramos' impressive grip on the UEFA Cup trophy and Spurs' chances of a second piece of silverware for the season.

Despite the obvious disappointment at the manner of their elimination from European competition, the team had little time to feel sorry for themselves as they travelled to Manchester to face City at Eastlands the following weekend with the emphasis firmly on improving their standing in the league. But despite Robbie Keane firing them into a one-goal lead at the break, City bounced back with goals from Stephen Ireland and Nedum Onuoha to condemn the visitors to yet another league defeat, their 12th in the league.

Next up for Spurs came the visit of title-chasing Chelsea who were also out for revenge following their defeat to their fellow Londoners in the Carling Cup Final just four weeks earlier. But having held the lead 1-0, 3-1 and 4-3 during a pulsating match at the Lane, Chelsea's challenge for the title was dealt a massive blow with just two minutes remaining when Robbie Keane curled home a stunning equaliser from outside the box to ensure a point for the home team. And Spurs could and perhaps should have taken all three points with the final whistle a matter of seconds away, only for the normally deadly Berbatov, who had already scored once earlier in the match, to miss the final goal-scoring opportunity.

A 2-0 win over Portsmouth followed, Berbatov providing an assist for Darren Bent to break the deadlock with just ten minutes remaining on the White Hart Lane clock, before Bent's fellow substitute Jamie O'Hara wrapped up a 2-0 victory a minute later. Two days later Berbatov travelled home to Bulgaria to collect his fourth Footballer of the Year award for 2007 as voted by the country's media outlets and reporters, leaving him just one award short of Bulgarian legend Hristo Stoichkov, who collected five awards during his own illustrious career. Berbatov returned to North London in time for the visit of Newcastle United to the Lane but Bulgaria's favourite sporting son was helpless to prevent Spurs crashing to a demoralising 4-1 defeat at the hands of the Geordie Army to leave the team languishing in mid-table obscurity.

And ahead of the team's trip north to face Mark Hughes' Blackburn Rovers outfit at Ewood Park, Berbatov, in an indication of his happiness at the club despite the continual conjecture surrounding his future and the team's inconsistent league form, revealed his delight with the way his and Robbie Keane's partnership had blossomed since joining the club in the summer of 2007: 'I'm very happy that our relationship is like that on the field. Obviously there are games when things are not working right but we know how to play with each other. When one is moving the other wants the ball, it's like a telepathic connection. That's what I like, he is a great technical player, he thinks with his head when he is playing and that's what I like most about him. Last season was great as well and this season we have proved again we can work together and understand each other.'

Berbatov struck the opening goal of the game with just six minutes on the clock, capitalising on some good link up play between Jenas and Steed Malbranque to volley home and give the team the best possible start, only for an equaliser from Norwegian winger Morten Gamst Pedersen to rob of them all three points.

Following the stalemate with Blackburn, Berbatov again travelled home to his homeland to receive a special Foreign Ministry award dedicated to him for his ambassadorial work on behalf of Bulgaria throughout the world. Speaking of the presentation, Bulgarian Foreign Minister, Ivaylo Kalfin, said: 'The interest towards Berbatov is extremely high. The last time the Foreign Ministry was so excited, was about the visit of the US state secretary Condoleezza Rice. Berbatov does his work in a perfect way, but the most valuable thing about him is that as a very successful Bulgarian he is a positive ambassador not only in the UK, but throughout the whole world.'

Berbatov meanwhile admitted his delight at receiving the award while also revealing his ambition to establish a foundation for children in the future: 'I'm very pleased with this prize. I don't like to speak too much, but I'll declare I have an idea to establish a Dimitar Berbatov foundation. I want to maintain talented children. I'm interested not only in footballers, but also in children with artistic talents.'

And speaking to *Sport* magazine on his return to England, Berbatov, in a demonstration of his apparent desire to remain a Spur under new manager Juande Ramos' stewardship, said: 'Of course, we have had some difficulties this season, but if we learn from our mistakes I think we can go forward. With the ability of the players we have, the future for Tottenham is bright. We must always aim to challenge the top four. The start of this season was difficult, but we have hope for next season. Winning the Carling Cup this year has given us hope. You have to have big ambition. I would lie if I say we don't think about the title at the start of the season. When I came, I knew that Liverpool, Man United, Arsenal and Chelsea were the big four and every year they fight for the title; but I was thinking why not go there and mess it all up? That hasn't happened, but we still have a good team – I'm sure we can surprise a lot of people next season.'

Yet another two points were dropped when

Middlesbrough visited the Lane and even another early opener from Berbatov couldn't prevent Spurs dropping further points on their travels north to face Steve Bruce's Wigan at the JJB Stadium. And after watching his team equalise to deny Berbatov the winner, Bruce coyly intimated that the naturally gifted eastern European reminded him of a certain Frenchman he had played alongside while at Manchester United, Eric Cantona: 'He's sheer class. He makes it look so easy. He reminds me of a top, top player.'

Croatia's highly-rated and gifted playmaker Luka Modric took his place in the directors' box for the visit of Bolton Wanderers to the Lane the following weekend, a £15.8 million transfer from Dinamo Zagreb having been agreed subject to the player passing his medical to show the ambition of Ramos to turn Spurs into a club capable of challenging the 'big four'. However, even the presence of one of Europe's most sought-after players couldn't inspire his future teammates to grind out a much-needed win against Gary Megson's team, as Ramos' men succumbed to a fourth 1-1 draw in succession.

And after the frustrating draw, Ramos admitted that even though he would prefer him to stay, Spurs would contemplate selling their Berbatov if a club matched the board's valuation and if it was in the best interests of the club to make the sale: 'We know the situation of Berbatov and we are calm about it. If a team comes along and pays the asking price the chairman wants, then possibly, yes, but we're delighted to have him here.'

Spurs ended their lacklustre run of five games without

a win in the team's penultimate match of the season at relegation-threatened Reading when Robbie Keane fired home the winner, his final goal as a Tottenham Hotspur player. And the team finished the season against Keane's future club, Liverpool at the Lane. However, to the disappointment of supporters hoping for a winning conclusion to an under-par league campaign, it was Liverpool who returned north with the points following a 2-0 win to condemn Spurs to an 11th place finish in the final league table.

Would this defeat be the final time the White Hart Lane faithful would see Berbatov wearing their famous white shirt? His former national team coach Hristo Stoichkov certainly thought so, suggesting that Berbatov would be the perfect signing for his former club Barcelona, especially if the rumours about Cameroon striker Samuel Eto'o departing Camp Nou were to be believed. Stoichkov enthused: 'If I was Barcelona president, I would sign Berbatov straight away.'

However, following a summer of transfer activity at White Hart Lane which saw players such as Keane, Pascal Chimbonda, Teemu Tainio, Steed Malbranque and Paul Robinson depart the North London club for pastures new, Berbatov returned to pre-season training at Spurs Lodge alongside a whole host of expensive and exciting new signings which suggested Ramos was intent on improving the team's fortunes in the 2008/09 season. In addition to Modric, PSV Eindhoven goalkeeper Heurelho Gomes, who had ended Spurs' UEFA Cup dreams the previous season, arrived to take the goalkeeper's jersey at the Lane, while the welcome mat was also rolled out for teenage sensation Giovani dos Santos who arrived for a somewhat modest fee of under £5 million from Catalan giants Barcelona. Ramos also signalled his intent to compete for the biggest names as he splashed out a massive £15 million to capture Blackburn's England winger David Bentley from Blackburn Rovers.

But after a pre-season which saw the team win seven out of their eight fixtures and also collect the prestigious Feyenoord Jubileum Tournament in Rotterdam, it appeared with the first match of the season on the horizon and with little apparent interest thus far in the transfer window, that the odds of Berbatov remaining in the capital were improving all the time. Ramos named the Bulgarian on the substitute bench for the season's curtain-raiser away at Middlesbrough. But it was to prove yet another disappointing start to the league campaign as a goal from defender David Wheater put Boro ahead before Berbatov was introduced to the fray in the hope of inspiring the team to a comeback. However, a goal from former Spurs striker Mido stretched Boro's lead and despite a late Robert Huth's own goal it was to prove another disappointing opening day at the office for Spurs as the home team triumphed 2-1.

With his future at the Lane still shrouded in doubt, Berbatov travelled to Zenitza in midweek to captain Bulgaria against Bosnia and Herzegovina in the first-ever meeting between the two nations. And putting the doubts and rumours over his club future to one side, he inspired his country to victory with his 40th and 41st goals in the national colours.

Back in England and one week after the disappointing defeat to Gareth Southgate's Teesiders, Tottenham lined up to face their first home game of the season hoping to make amends as Sunderland made the long journey south, looking for their own first win of the new campaign after losing their opening fixture at home to Liverpool. And with the speculation beginning to grow over a possible transfer bid from Manchester United for Berbatov, Ramos decided to leave the unsettled Bulgarian out of his squad completely for the Mackems' visit to the Lane. Speaking before the game, Ramos outlined his reasons for leaving his number one striker out of the match day squad: 'I needed to wait and speak to the player when he returned from international duty and then make a decision about whether or not he was right to play in this game.'

Without Berbatov, Spurs went on to lose to Roy Keane's men as their disappointing start to the new season continued. With the ever-faithful fans around White Hart Lane becoming increasingly frustrated with the will he/won't he situation regarding Berbatov's future, sporting director Damien Comolli came out only days before the transfer window deadline and told Sky Sports News he hoped the Bulgarian would be going nowhere: 'I hope so, of course. He's a very good player and, as Juande [Ramos] has said many times, we're delighted he's with us. I don't really want to comment about speculation, but we just hope he's going to stay.'

With the transfer deadline now fast approaching, Ramos, having lost Robbie Keane to Liverpool earlier in the summer and now facing the possibility of losing his other top striker, splashed the cash again, this time raiding Spartak Moscow for their prolific international striker Roman Pavlyuchenko, who had performed so well for Russia during their impressive charge to the semi-finals of the 2008 European Championship finals. However, the question on everybody's lips at White Hart Lane and Old Trafford remained unanswered. Which club would Dimitar Berbatov be playing his football for on September 2, 2009? Even Gus Poyet, Ramos' assistant appeared unsure telling *Sky Sports*: 'You will know tomorrow.'

CHAPTER 12

WHITE HART TO THEATRE OF DREAMS

'This is a key signing. Dimitar is one of the best and most exciting strikers in world football.'

SIR ALEX FERGUSON

1 September 2008 will be a day remembered in Manchester for many years to come. Having tracked Tottenham Hotspur's cultured and prolific striker Dimitar Berbatov since his days at Bayer Leverkusen, it appeared that Manchester United manager Sir Alex Ferguson stood on the brink of losing his number one transfer target to bitter rivals Manchester City, who were themselves enjoying new-found wealth after being taken over by the Abu Dhabi United Group.

With only hours of the summer transfer window remaining, City manager Mark Hughes, himself a Manchester United legend who had served Ferguson with the utmost distinction between 1988 and 1995, said City had made a British transfer record bid for Berbatov of over £30 million: 'We have made an offer, I think it's been agreed between ourselves and Tottenham and it's really about the boy making a decision. I'm as stunned and excited by this as the fans are.'

All the signs pointed to Berbatov heading to Eastlands to join Hughes and the blue half of Manchester's revolution. But, within hours of revealing City's bid, Sky were reporting that City, in a spectacular move, had completed the signing of Real Madrid and Brazil superstar Robinho, leaving the door open for United to tie up a deal for Tottenham's number one star. And finally, with a large collection of excited fans gathered outside Old Trafford awaiting the outcome of the Berbatov deal and the clock ticking down towards the midnight deadline, a statement from a United spokesman confirmed a deal had been struck between United and Tottenham and that the Bulgarian had agreed terms on a club record £30.75 million with Frazier Campbell moving in the opposite direction on a season-long loan. Fergie, after a long wait, finally had his man. His new number nine. His new Eric Cantona.

And upon unveiling his new superstar signing, a delighted Ferguson revealed he had in fact tried to sign Berbatov two years earlier when the Bulgarian had signed for the White Hart Lane club in an £11 million deal.

Berbatov meanwhile revealed in his first interview with *MUTV* since completing his 'dream move' to the *Theatre of Dreams* on a four-year contract, his excitement and desire to help the champions win even more silverware: 'I've handled expectation and pressure throughout my life – I'm not scared of that. That's why I'm here. The most important thing is to enjoy myself, help the team win more trophies and to thank the fans. If I do that and show what I can do like I did at Tottenham, I don't think there'll be any problems. I hope my peak years are still to come. I'm 27 and now is my time. This is perhaps the last step in my career and the biggest club in the world.'

And after spurning City's offer to join United Berbatov admitted that it had never crossed his mind to join Mark Hughes' new regime across town, and that he only ever had one intention. Having departed north London himself during the summer to join United biggest rivals Liverpool, Berbatov's former striking partner Robbie Keane, who spent two highly successful seasons playing alongside the Bulgarian at White Hart Lane, expressed his belief that Berbatov would prove a superb signing for Ferguson.

'It was no secret that he was going to go there,' he said. 'Everybody knew that Berba was going to go to Manchester United. It's a fantastic move for him, but it's a massive one for Man United because he is a top, top player. I have seen that at first hand and he will be a massive addition to the Man United squad. I am sure Berba wants to be a better player and he wants to win things, and I think that's the reason he went to Manchester United.'

After helping Bulgaria to a 2-2 draw with Montenegro in his country's opening World Cup 2010 qualifying match, Berbatov's first outing in United colours would, fittingly perhaps, witness him lining up against his former colleague Keane in a baptism of fire against Liverpool at Anfield. Ahead of the game, Berbatov admitted that he would be feeling the nerves a little before running out for the first time as a United player: 'I might be nervous

247

because it's a new team, new players, a new atmosphere. But hopefully with the help of my team-mates I can find my place in the side and help the team with my goals. It will be strange to play against Robbie, but it will also be nice. I have good memories of playing alongside him. It was a good partnership. Everything comes to an end but I will be glad to see him again.'

But despite taking just three minutes to show the travelling fans exactly why the club had broken their transfer record to sign him, by delightfully setting up Carlos Tevez to give United the lead, Berbatov was helpless to prevent his new team-mates slipping to a first league defeat against Liverpool since 2004, courtesy of an unfortunate own goal from Wes Brown and a late winner from substitute Ryan Babel. And, after picking up a knee injury in the defeat, Berbatov would have to wait a little longer to line-up for his first Champions League appearance since Liverpool eliminated his Leverkusen team on their way to glory in Istanbul in 2005.

But despite the disappointment of missing out on the match with Villarreal, Berbatov revealed to Bulgarian television station BTV how happy he was at the prospect of playing in the competition again: 'I'm very happy that I will play in the Champions League again. I've been dreaming for this moment for a long time. For me it is amazing to hear the tournament's theme while I'm on the field, but unfortunately, this will not happen tomorrow. Sir Alex and me decided that it would be better not to risk it, because I got a little problem during the Liverpool game.'

And without their new record signing, the reigning

champions were frustrated and held to a 0-0 draw at Old Trafford by their Spanish opponents as Europe's premiere competition kicked off once again. A fit-again Berbatov returned to the starting XI for United's second huge league clash in a week as Ferguson's men travelled to West London to face Chelsea at Stamford Bridge. And with just 18 minutes played, Berbatov, who started the match alongside England's first choice striker Wayne Rooney, forced Blues keeper Petr Cech into a save which he could only parry into the path of Ji-sung Park, who in turn fired the ball home to give United the lead. However, for the second league match in a row, United were unable to hold onto their slender lead as once again a substitute, this time Salomon Kalou, took advantage of some sloppy defending to head the equaliser and preserve new Chelsea manager Luiz Felipe Scolari's unbeaten start.

Berbatov joined a number of his first team colleagues in sitting out United's comfortable 3-1 victory over Middlesbrough in the Carling Cup third round at Old Trafford before returning to the starting line-up for the visit of Bolton alongside Carlos Tevez as he sought to break his goal-scoring duck against United's Lancashire rivals. A penalty from Ronaldo followed by a superb finish from Tevez's replacement, Rooney, wrapped up the points for United and despite missing a couple of opportunities to open his account for the Red Devils, Berbatov maintained he was just happy the team had returned to winning ways: 'I really wanted to score a goal. But the three points are the most important thing and we were the better team today. We scored two goals but missed four or five chances. I'm happy with how I'm playing, particularly after today. The game was good for me. I didn't take my chances so hopefully in the future I will score. I think today was a big improvement from myself and from the team. I'm working really hard to help the team and so I can develop a better understanding with everyone. I'm sure that will happen.'

United returned to Champions League action on the back of the victory over Bolton with a trip to Danish outfit Aalborg BK and this time Berbatov was fit to take his place in Ferguson's starting line-up. But on the day of the match, former Tottenham and England manager publicly attacked Berbatov in a newspaper interview with *The Sun* claiming the Bulgarian was largely to blame for the north London club's poor start to the season which had seen them slip to the foot of the Premier League table. However, despite Venables' criticism, Berbatov kicked off the match with Aalborg interested only in helping his new team to victory. After missing a glorious early opportunity to open the scoring, Berbatov watched as his strike partner Rooney finished smartly to give United the lead midway through the first half. And with ten minutes of the second half played, the moment Berbatov and the United fans had been waiting for finally arrived. Pouncing on a dreadful mistake on the edge of the area by Aalborg defender Thomas Augustinussen, Berbatov set himself and rammed home his first goal for the club in ruthless style to double United's advantage. The forward then doubled his tally with ten minutes of the match remaining as he acrobatically volleyed home a cross from Cristiano Ronaldo to wrap up a comfortable 3-0 win for the holders.

After the win, Ronaldo told Sky Sports of his happiness with Berbatov's contribution to the team's win: 'It's good. It's good for Berba to score his first goals for Manchester. He played good. It's always good for the forwards to score to keep the confidence high.'

In an interview with the *Daily Star*, Berbatov revealed how he was feeling settled and happy with his move to the reigning Premier League and European champions: 'If I am not happy here, I cannot be happy anywhere. Everything is like Ryan Giggs once said. He was here from the beginning and he doesn't want to be anywhere else. I am here. I don't want to go anywhere else. I find myself sitting at home sometimes, thinking: Hey, I am at Manchester United! I am the happiest guy. It is a wonderful thing. But you must keep fighting in every game. I was relieved, obviously.

'I was disappointed to miss my first chance because sometimes in games you get only the one chance. It was frustrating but I just kept trying and, of course, in the end I scored two. The pressure is always there and I hope I can deal with that with the help of my team-mates. I didn't celebrate my first goal because I was still angry and disappointed with myself over the first one I missed. I was embarrassed. For a guy who has been bought for all this money, I must take these chances so that is why I was angry.'

A confident 2-0 win over Blackburn Rovers at Ewood Park followed before the players set off on international duty with their respective countries. First up for Berbatov and his Bulgarian teammates in a qualifying double-header came the visit from World Cup winners Italy. The team managed to hold the *Azzurri* to a respectable 0-0 draw in Sofia, but their hopes of qualifying for the 2010 tournament in South Africa were dented when Georgia, led by Berbatov's former coach at Leverkusen, Klaus Toppmoller, held Bulgaria to a goalless stalemate in Tbilisi, Bulgaria's third draw from three matches.

United welcomed West Bromich Albion to Old Trafford on the players' return from international duty and for Berbatov the 4-0 victory would prove an occasion to remember. Rooney opened the scoring, latching onto Berbatov's through ball to fire home past Albion keeper Scott Carson before Ronaldo doubled the lead. And in the 72nd minute, the moment for which Berbatov had been waiting finally arrived, when a cross from Portuguese winger Nani eluded Albion's defence to allow the Bulgarian to mercilessly lash home his first league goal for the club before Nani added a fourth to round off an easy 4-0 win.

Next up, United welcomed Gordon Strachan's Scottish champions Celtic to Old Trafford for a Champions League match labelled the 'Battle of Britain'. But in a particularly one-sided affair, two close-range strikes from Berbatov and a third from Rooney ensured United remained on course to qualify with games to spare for the knockout stages of the competition. After inspiring the team to the brink of qualification for the second round, Berbatov insisted he was still aiming to improve despite his recent good form: 'I will improve, that's why I'm here, that's why I came here. I'm at the biggest club and I try hard in training and you can see in the games that everything is working right at the moment When you are here you don't have time to hide during games, you have to work hard and always give one hundred per cent in the game and that's what I'm doing. In the past I lacked that in some games.'

United returned to league action with a visit to Merseyside to face Everton at Goodison Park but not for the first time travelled back down the M62 motorway disappointed as Darren Fletcher's opener was only enough to secure a point when Marouane Fellaini's header ensured a share of the spoils for David Moyes' men. On the back of the draw with Everton, United welcomed Gianfranco Zola's West Ham to Old Trafford as Ferguson's men looked to get straight back to winning ways. Ronaldo set them on their way with his first of the afternoon before Berbatov displayed a piece of outrageous skill on the goal line to leave James Collins dumbfounded before squaring the ball for Ronaldo to double his tally for the day.

After witnessing Berbatov's moment of magic, Ferguson told Sky Sports News of his desire to see his team utilise the Bulgarian's talents more often: 'Some of his awareness and passing ability in the last third of the field has been outstanding. I still don't think we're using him enough. On Wednesday I wanted to see how the combination of Berbatov and Tevez was together. Carlos was so wound up to do well himself that they became two different parts. I think it will be far better tomorrow, if I pick him.'

Ferguson retained Berbatov for the visit of newly-promoted Hull while Tevez dropped down to the bench to be replaced by Wayne Rooney, but the change of personnel did little to limit United's immense goal-scoring threat as the team raced into a 4-1 lead. And despite a late fight-back from Phil Brown's high-flying Tigers outfit, United held on to win 4-3 and continue their charge back towards the top end of the table.

The day after the victory, Berbatov's former chairman at Spurs, Daniel Levy, who had only recently sacked Juande Ramos as manager following the club's terrible start to the season, spoke openly for the first time about the striker's departure from White Hart Lane and was critical of him.

Meanwhile, Ferguson named Berbatov and a number of his senior players on the bench for the trip to Celtic Park to face the Scottish champion's in the Champions League in midweek but the decision appeared to have backfired when, with the match entering its final stages, Scott McDonald's solitary strike separated the two teams. But a late header by the ever-green Ryan Giggs, following a sustained period of dominance, ensured the away team returned to Manchester with a deserved point.

Three days later however, United travelled to North London to face their great rivals Arsenal at Emirates Stadium but despite putting the ball into an empty net early on in the first half, Berbatov saw his strike chalked off for offside. And two wonderful goals from French forward Samir Nasri condemned United to only their second league defeat of the season despite Rafael's late strike giving them hope of a share of the spoils. A 1-0 League Cup win over Queen Park Rangers at Old Trafford followed before United ruthlessly despatched

Premier League new boys Stoke City 5-0 in front of their adoring supporters. Cristiano Ronaldo fired home two free-kicks, bringing up his 100th goal since arriving as a replacement for David Beckham in 2003, while further goals from Michael Carrick, Berbatov – turning home a Tevez cross – and a strike from teenage forward Danny Welbeck wrapped up a ruthless mauling of Tony Pulis' set-piece specialists.

Before the match, Berbatov took time out to express his happiness that his former club Tottenham, under the guidance of new manager Harry Redknapp, had finally started to turn around their dreadful start to the season. Speaking to *The Sun*, Berbatov said: 'I will always have special feelings for Tottenham. They showed me the way in English football. I will never have anything bad to say about the club. I watch every game they play. I was just surprised the team got off to such a bad start because Juande Ramos was a very good coach. Now Harry Redknapp has come in, a very experienced manager, and I am pleased they are going up the table.'

Two goal-less away draws against Aston Villa and Villarreal followed, the 0-0 draw in the Spanish team's El Madrigal Stadium confirming United's qualification for the knock-out stages of the Champions League. And despite his absence from both matches after picking up a hamstring injury during his country's humiliating 6-1 friendly defeat at the hands of Serbia the previous week, the Bulgarian admitted just how satisfying it was to be playing for a manager of the stature and experience of Ferguson, and that he was more than willing to accept the need for rotation that having a hugely talented squad brings with it: 'It is enjoyable. Sometimes you get a little bit nervous around him because obviously he is Sir Alex. You don't know what to say or do sometimes. He is a really nice guy. He speaks with you when necessary, or sometimes he raises his voice to make his point clear. It is up to Sir Alex who plays. Everybody wants to play and I think in some games we could even play all four strikers. But of course there will be rotation and it is difficult when you don't play some games. That is football.

'I am still working on everything. Everything is new to me. I am still working on my training sessions and my performance in games. But I think, for now, things are going according to plan. I am working hard and fighting for my place. Sir Alex is in charge and you must prove to him in every training session and every game. And I am trying to do that.'

United made a welcome return to winning ways in the season's first derby match against Mark Hughes' big-spending City at Eastlands, Wayne Rooney prodding home the only goal of the game to secure the red half of the city the bragging rights for the best part of six months until the reverse fixture between the two teams. Berbatov made a surprise return to the starting line-up for the short trip across the city, but was again rested for the astounding 5-3 League Cup win over Blackburn at Old Trafford in midweek.

Centre-back Nemanja Vidic made himself the hero as United snatched a last gasp 1-0 win over Sunderland at Old Trafford to keep on the trail of early pace-setters Liverpool and Chelsea before the team completed their Champions League group fixtures with an underwhelming 2-2 draw with Aalborg at the Theatre of Dreams. The following weekend marked the first return to White Hart Lane for Berbatov since his controversial record-breaking move from North London to Old Trafford in the summer. And with the Spurs faithful expected to give their former idol a torrent of abuse upon his return, Lilywhites' manager Harry Redknapp revealed that he didn't expect the level to be as excessive as that former Spurs favourite Sol Campbell received upon his return to the Lane on numerous occasions:

'Getting stick is part of the game. You leave a club and you get a bit of grief when you go back. We accept that, and it happens. As long as it's not racist abuse or anything they're entitled to shout, jeer or boo or whatever they want to do. Berbatov might get some stick but he won't get the type of abuse Sol got, which was definitely out of order. Alex would tell them that there is only one way to keep them quiet and that is to put the ball in the back of the net. That is what I would say to a player. He was a good player here and the club got fantastic money for him.'

Ferguson revealed he had no doubts that Berbatov would cope with the anticipated heated reception from his former supporters, while also backing his number nine to eventually shine at Old Trafford: 'Dimitar is a great player. We are still getting used to using him properly. You can see the quality. He is fantastic. There are very few players who can produce moments like he does in games. It can decide them. He is going to get the reception we expect. It is part of modern-day society and is never going to change. Berbatov knows he is going to get a lot of abuse from the fans. If it had been anyone apart from United it would not have caused as much of a furore. They still regret selling Carrick to us, which is the biggest problem. But they wanted to sell him to us, so I can't see how they blame us for that. They got a good deal on that last day as well, getting Fraizer Campbell in the bargain. They really milked it well.'

And how correct Ferguson was. For every time the Bulgarian touched the ball during the match he received the expected barracking from the raucous and angered home support. And unfortunately for Berbatov he was unable to ram the taunts of the fans back down their throats as he struggled to impose himself on a game which ended scoreless.

Next up for United came a trip to the Far East and the challenge of adding the FIFA World Club Championship to the Premier League and Champions League trophies already safely locked away in the silverware cabinet back at Old Trafford. But after picking up a virus upon the squad's arrival in Japan which prevented him from taking part in any training, Berbatov was forced to sit out both the 5-3 semi-final win over Gamba Osaka and the 1-0 victory over surprise Copa Libertadores winners LDU Quito as United comfortably wrapped up another trophy to add to their burgeoning haul for the year.

The squad returned home to England in time for Christmas and made the short journey to Stoke-On-Trent on Boxing Day looking to pick up another vital three points in the club's chase to narrow the gap at the top of the Premier League table. However, the game looked to be destined for stalemate until Ferguson sacrificed defender John O'Shea and replaced him with the fit-again Berbatov. And following the sending off of young Stoke defender Andy Wilkinson for two cautions, Berbatov nipped in to cross the ball to the back post for Carlos Tevez to apply the simplest of finishes with seven minutes remaining to give United another vital late win. And it proved a very happy festive period for the Berbatov family as Dimitar returned home to Bulgaria to attend a ceremony on 27 December where he received a staggering fifth Bulgarian Player of the Year award to put the seal on a fantastic year.

The final match of 2008 saw United welcome Gareth Southgate's Middlesbrough to Old Trafford. And in a totally one-sided fixture dominated in its entirety by the Red Devils, a solitary goal from Berbatov proved enough to reduce Liverpool's lead at the top of the Premier League table to seven points with United also enjoying two games in hand over their bitter northern rivals.

United started the new year with an FA Cup tie against financially-stricken Championship club Southampton at St. Mary's Stadium on the south coast. But not even the magic of the FA Cup could provide Jan Poortvliet's youthful team with a much-needed boost as United romped to an easy 3-0 victory. Before the match, Ferguson had felt the need to publicly defend his latest superstar signing, Berbatov, against more widespread criticism of the Bulgarian's style, telling the *Daily Star*: 'I don't agree with the criticism that he slows us down. I don't agree with that at all. In fact, I don't think we have used him enough. He's fine. It's like everything else. Whenever a player comes here, if there's a way of criticising him, they will find it. They are saying he's this and he's that. But his stats are incredible. He did more running [against Middlesbrough] on Monday night than any other front player, including Rooney. I think it's the languid style of his that's the problem. The stats, though, would surprise you. They don't surprise me. I don't always pay attention to stats, to be honest, yet it's good to know in this case.'

A surprising 1-0 defeat to another Championship club, Derby County, followed in the first leg of the League Cup semi-final at Pride Park, as United's preparations for the forthcoming clash with fellow title chasers Chelsea took a knock. And ahead of the huge clash of the Premier League heavyweights, Berbatov told MUTV that he had settled in to life in the north with ease, contrary to rumours which suggested otherwise: 'People talk about the north and the south but I don't make comparisons like that, I am just interested in my football. People say it is not sunny here and it rains all the time but that doesn't bother me. I like it the way it is. In fact, I like it better here. I am not a guy who looks for places with a lot of people and traffic. London was crazy anyway, so I used to live out of town. Here it is more peaceful. But the city is secondary to the team I play for. Now I play for the biggest team in the world, so it doesn't matter where I live. I am very happy and things are going well. My dream was to come here, now I can see how the biggest stars are working and I can compare and measure myself against the best. I come into work and enjoy training, then I go home but I just want to go to bed and then start training again. I enjoy sharing jokes. But when we work it is serious. We have very important games ahead of us and we need to prepare for them.'

And rising to the big occasion as he so often has in the past, Berbatov inspired United to a comfortable 3-0 victory over their title rivals, as he flicked on Ryan Giggs' corner into the path of Vidic to head home the opener just before the half-time interval. Rooney added a second with just under 30 minutes remaining before the Bulgarian wrapped up a massively satisfying victory when he smashed home Ronaldo's free-kick in the dying minutes to narrow Liverpool's lead at the top of the table to just five points after the Merseysiders dropped points with a 0-0 draw at Stoke.

Cristiano Ronaldo paraded his FIFA World Player of the Year award ahead of the club's next match against Wigan and another goal from Rooney ensured the team narrowed the gap even further on Liverpool to just two points with a hard-fought win at Old Trafford. Meanwhile, having been referred to by many during his short time at Old Trafford as United's 'new Eric Cantona', Berbatov admitted that the pressure of such a comparison wasn't one that he relished: 'It's not good to be compared to a legend, as it brings more pressure. I have my own style. I play my own way. I want to be known for that, rather than the comparison to be made. And there is no comparison. I have a long way to go.'

And in the very next game Berbatov proved his worth to United as a player in his own right when he popped up to head home another last minute winner to secure all three points against Bolton at the Reebok Stadium. United's fifth win in a row also marked the first time the club had occupied top spot in the Premier League during the 2008/09 season. Ferguson again rested Berbatov for the visit of newly appointed Nigel Clough's Derby County for the second leg of the League Cup semi-final and United coped comfortably without him as the club booked their place in another final with a 4-2 victory.

However, the deadly Bulgarian was back in the starting line-up for the FA Cup tie with his old side Spurs at Old Trafford the following weekend and celebrated his forthcoming 28th birthday early by firing home a fantastic winning goal to send his new club through to the fifth round of the FA Cup and keep their quest to win all five major trophies alive.

So what does the future hold for Dimitar Berbatov? Will he win the silverware he so desperately craves at Old Trafford? Will he etch his name into Old Trafford folklore and become a legend spoken of in the same breath as Duncan Edwards, Bobby Charlton, Denis Law, Bryan Robson, Eric Cantona and Ryan Giggs? Will he ever represent his country on the biggest international stage of all, the World Cup Finals? They are all questions that cannot be answered at this moment in time. However, he certainly possesses the attributes to achieve whatever he wants to achieve. His fantastic natural ability coupled with having arguably the world's best current manager guiding him and a squad bristling with some of the world's finest players, should certainly help him achieve whatever he wants.

One thing is for certain though. At some point before he retires from the game, Berbatov intends to wear the shirt of CSKA Sofia again. And he hopes to wear it alongside his friend and countryman Martin Petrov. In an interview with the *Mail on Sunday* in December 2007, his agent Emil Dantchev admitted as much: 'They have made plans to play together in the future. They are looking towards the end of their careers and being reunited at CSKA before they quit the game. They have made Bulgarians very proud. They are not the only Bulgarians playing in England now, but there will be many more going over to play in the Premier League because of them.'